Also from

Making the Choice
When Typical School Doesn't Fit Your Atypical Child

Forging Paths
Beyond Traditional Schooling

If This is a Gift, Can I Send it Back?
Surviving in the Land of the Gifted and Twice Exceptional

Learning in the 21st Century
How to Connect, Collaborate, and Create

How to Work and Homeschool
Practical Tips, Advice, and Strategies from Parents

Educating Your Gifted Child
How One Public School Teacher Embraced Homeschooling

Self-Directed Learning
Documentation and Life Stories

Gifted, Bullied, Resilient
A Brief Guide for Smart Families

Writing Your Own Script
A Parent's Role in the Gifted Child's Social Development

Micro-Schools
Creating Personalized Learning on a Budget

Your Rainforest Mind
A Guide to the Well-Being of Gifted Adults and Youth

From Home Education to Higher Education
A Guide for Recruiting, Assessing, and Supporting Homeschooled Applicants

Coming Soon from GHF Press
www.giftedhomeschoolers.org/ghf-press/

Kathleen Humble
Gifted Myths

Joy Navan
Gifted Elders

Celi Trépanier
Gifted Stories

Boost:
12 Effective Ways to Lift Up Our Twice-Exceptional Children

By Kelly Hirt

Edited by Sarah J. Wilson

Published by GHF Press
A Division of Gifted Homeschoolers Forum
3701 Pacific Ave. SE - PMB #609
Olympia, WA 98501

ISBN-13: 978-0692980101 (GHF Press)
ISBN-10: 0692980105

Cover design by Shawn Keehne
www.shawnkeehne.com • skeehne@mac.com

To my past, present, and future students.

Contents

Acknowledgments

Unless someone like you cares a whole awful lot, nothing is going to get better. It's not.

~Dr. Seuss, *The Lorax*

When I came across Diane Kennedy, Rebecca Banks, and Temple Grandin's book, *Bright Not Broken: Gifted Kids, ADHD, and Autism*, I was searching for answers as to why my intelligent son was struggling in his neighborhood school. After reading that book, I realized that it was not my son who needed to change, but our approach toward his learning. I owe these ladies a debt of gratitude that I can only repay by helping other children and families.

I have such gratitude for everyone at GHF: Gifted Homeschoolers Forum. GHF has been a lifeline for me as I discovered and grew more comfortable with homeschooling. They showed me that my professional life as a teacher and my passion for homeschooling could be brought together to educate others.

Much of the support and strength that I receive comes from parents whom I have never met in person, but who share my cause and champion my writing. I am grateful.

I want to acknowledge the hard-working teachers who keep learning to benefit all of your students.

I want to thank Diane. Your belief in me as a mother, writer, and educator, even when I questioned myself, is the reason this book is completed. To my precious son, you are my greatest teacher.

Finally, I honor the homeschooling families who take on the full responsibility of educating their children.

It's no use going back to yesterday, because I was a different person then.

~Lewis Carroll, *Alice's Adventures in Wonderland*

My Story

I was an elementary teacher for fourteen years before I became a parent. During that time, parents sought my advice about homework struggles, friendship skills, bedtime chaos, and instilling responsibility at home. I was happy to share my expertise and they thanked me for my suggestions. I was convinced that I knew about children and parenting—before I became a parent, naturally.

I had received my MA in Curriculum Development, mentored student teachers, and was involved in curriculum adoption teams and leadership roles. I considered myself an effective teacher. I could prove that my students made impressive gains; however, I usually had at least one student each year who stumped me.

These students struck me as quirky, intense, or complicated. While I had been trained to work with various learning styles, these unique students pushed me beyond my education. The only thing that seemed consistent about these learners was just how different they were from my typical six- and seven-year-old students. The more I discovered about them, the more questions I had:

- How could a student with an impressive vocabulary and skill for storytelling be unable to read?

- Why would a seven-year-old with so many interests and a desire to share his passions refuse to put his ideas down on paper?

- Why was a first grader, who fixated on tiny leaves that blew into our classroom or was mesmerized by loose threads in the carpet—seemingly unable to focus—able to provide amazing insight after our daily read aloud?

- Why did a child who trusted me suddenly become agitated, wanting nothing to do with me or his classmates?

Sometimes, holding a conversation proved challenging for these students. Their passions sabotaged their ability to have reciprocal discussions. They often did not make eye contact. The sound of a pencil sharpener across the room could require them to restart their story. Their classmates grew tired of the one-sided conversations and formed friendships with children more predictable in temperament and age-appropriate interests.

Physical space seemed to be important. While some of these learners went to extremes to avoid physical closeness, others sought contact by leaning against students in line or squeezing an unsuspecting classmate. These particular students often needed to move more, making excuses to get scissors, a tissue, or another drink of water.

The other students avoided these students who seemed unpredictable with their moods, gestures, or words. Recess was stressful and lonely for many of these unique children. Perhaps my own confusion influenced the other students more than I realized.

These kids seemed to visit the principal's office more than others, perhaps attempting to find a private place to read or avoid the commotion of our energetic classroom. Specialists grew frustrated after unsuccessfully trying to make PE or music go smoother.

I wanted to help, but I did not know what to do. I knew we needed something different for these kids. After they graduated from my class, I would hope that their new teachers would seek answers to the unanswered questions.

That was the beginning of my quest, but my true education began only once I realized that my child was *one of these children*: a child who confused those entrusted to educate him. I expected my years as a teacher would help, but they did not.

When my son was a toddler, I often read parenting books. He seemed to fly past the typical milestones. He walked and ran early, built complicated structures, and played advanced games. Although he did not speak early, once he started, he did so using complete sentences, as if he had waited until he was confident that he could do it correctly.

As a mother and an experienced educator, I was thrilled when his skills were advanced. I had seen students struggle and I knew that was hard for children and their families. I figured school would be easy for my son, and was excited for him to start. This was my beloved profession, after all, and I knew he would feel the same way about school as I had.

During his preschool years, he developed intensities which concerned me. He needed an extreme amount of attention, had difficulty calming his mind and body, and grew increasingly stubborn when situations did not go as planned. He loved when I volunteered in his class, but was intolerant if I acknowledged his classmates. Friendship issues became the daily topic of discussion with his teachers. I tried to convince myself that these troubles would go away once he was in kindergarten. I expected that he would meet other students like him, and his needs would be met.

Unfortunately, school was not the easy road that I had predicted. Like many gifted children with unidentified disabilities, mine struggled, not because the academics were hard, but because of all the other components that made up his school experience: the classroom noise, crowded halls, lunchroom smells, friendship issues, repetition of already-covered material, number of transitions—the expectation that everyone march to the same beat.

I remember a particular exchange with my son's first grade teacher. She compared a drawing of an owl that my son had done and another picture completed by a different student.

"This is the owl that your son did in ten minutes and this is one that another student did, following my instructions for forty minutes."

Confused, I said, "They both look the same."

"Yes. But your son didn't follow my directions." Her voice indicated that I should have understood her disappointment.

I shook my head. "No, he did it a different way, a faster way, and it looks just the same."

During his first grade year, we learned that my gifted son was impacted by social and motor delays. Furthermore, sensory issues and executive functioning interfered with his success at school. This is when we learned about twice-exceptionality. I began to understand that my son was living at the far ends of a bell curve. Nothing seemed "normal" and everything was extreme. This explanation allowed me to help my son and, in turn, help more of my students by recognizing characteristics that I had previously misunderstood. I set out to learn more about twice-exceptional children and their unique needs.

As we discovered more about twice-exceptional learners, we shared our discoveries with my son's teachers and school administration. Despite our attempts to educate his educators, discussions similar to the owl project continued. His giftedness was ignored, even doubted, and his daily struggles were highlighted.

After four years and seven teachers, we reluctantly chose homeschooling. I say "reluctantly" because, as a veteran public school teacher, I never expected to homeschool my son. I believe in the institution of public school. I know many hard-working, well-intentioned teachers who want to do well by their students; however, despite good teachers and decent schools, some students cannot thrive in a traditional setting. My child seems to be one of those students.

Surprisingly, my family's struggles with our neighborhood school and decision to homeschool have made me a better classroom teacher. I understand parents who advocate for their children and now consider the many ways students can be successful. It is my job, not students', to change my awareness and increase my strategies.

In order to connect with other parents, I started a blog (MyTwiceBakedPotato.com). I quickly realized that I was not alone, as many readers shared similar frustrations.

- *Although my kindergartener can read at a sixth grade level, she is forced to sit through lessons about identifying the letters and sounds of the alphabet. She cries daily about school.*

- *My son's teacher sent him to the principal for "smart talk" because he tried showing her a quicker way to do the math problem on the board. He was told he'd get challenging math when he controlled his behavior.*

- *During a meeting with the principal, it was said that my son was lazy and spoiled. My son is six and highly gifted in the area of science, but he just hates to write.*

- *I was told that if I made home boring, my child would want to come to class. He wasn't allowed to go to his GT class because his behavior in class was not gifted.*

Not isolated complaints, I read similar situations on Facebook forums, other blogs, and emails or comments from my own readers. We must do something.

Through my experiences as a classroom teacher, writer, and mother, I have collected twelve themes that I see as critical to the success of twice-exceptional children. For the purpose of this book, I will call them strategies, but they are more than that. *Boost: 12 Effective Ways to Lift Up Our Twice-Exceptional Children* encompasses tried techniques, new approaches, and a positive way of thinking to support twice-exceptional learners.

I wrote *Boost* with two audiences in mind: educators and parents. If you are a classroom teacher, this book will help you better understand all of your students, not just the typical learners. Teachers, I have been you. I am you. I know the demands of your job. I know that if you did not take your responsibility to reach all students seriously, you would not have chosen this profession. Thus, your principal and support staff must also learn to understand these children, so you can receive the support you and your students need.

The second group, parent, means specifically those families advocating for children in traditional classrooms and those who have chosen homeschooling. Reading these twelve strategies will shift your thinking about your child's potential for learning. I certainly would have benefited from this information when I felt lost.

Let's challenge previously accepted thinking and focus on a positive approach that will boost your twice-exceptional learners.

Nothing is impossible; the word itself says I'm possible!
~Audrey Hepburn

Frequently Asked Questions about Twice-Exceptional Children

Understanding is the first steps to acceptance, and only with acceptance can there be recovery.

~JK Rowling

Many people remain unfamiliar with the unique needs of twice-exceptional (2e) learners. This book is meant to start that discussion for some, increase awareness for others, and help educators and parents support these children with the use of positive and effective strategies.

When I speak about 2e children and issues, I often get the same questions, some of which I have answered below.

Q. What does twice-exceptional (2e) mean?

A. "Twice exceptional" means that a child is both gifted and has a disability (educational, social, emotional, and/or behavioral). Many identified 2e students attend gifted classes and receive special education services with an IEP (Individualized Educational Plan). Because the disability may mask the giftedness or the giftedness disguise the disability, many students remain unidentified.

Q. What is asynchronous development?

A. The National Association for Gifted Children defines asynchrony as "disparate rates of intellectual, emotional, and physical rates of growth or development often displayed by gifted children."[1]

An asynchronous child may have an extensive vocabulary, but have trouble reading. She might do complicated math in her head, but is unable to show her work on paper. She could have a passion for a specific scientific topic or an interest in Greek mythology, but not able to ride a bike or maintain friendships.

Q. How are 2e children different from gifted children?

A. While both groups have high IQs, 2e children possess unevenly dispersed strengths, which may cause the influencing adults in their lives to doubt their giftedness. These children's giftedness often masks their disabilities, as it may allow them to perform at an acceptable level, though nowhere close to their potential.

Twice-exceptional children are complex. Often, the higher their intelligence, the greater their asynchronous development, the greater the impact from their intensities. When left unrecognized or underserved, complicated behaviors, frustration, and self-esteem issues often arise. Think of 2e as living simultaneously at the ends of a bell curve. Little about a 2e kid resides in the middle.

Although 2e students are gifted learners, not all gifted students are 2e. We readily accept the idea that academically gifted students exist in our schools. Unfortunately, most educators not only lack training about twice-exceptional students, but are unfamiliar with the term or the very existence of 2e children.

Q. Are "intensities" the same as "asynchronous development"?

A. The terms are not the same, but are related. The Theory of Overexcitability, proposed by Kazimierz Dabrowski, a Polish psychologist, psychiatrist, and physician, suggests that some individuals have heightened sensitivities, awareness, and intensity in one or more of five areas: Psychomotor, Sensual, Intellectual, Imaginational, and Emotional.[2] Twice-exceptional children are often impacted to varying degrees by more than one of these areas. The more gifted the child, the more issues which may be attributed to uneven development.

Q. Don't smart kids have it easy in school?

A. Unfortunately, people still erroneously believe that gifted kids are always the self-motivated, quick-to-learn, ready-to-help leaders in the classroom. Many feel that gifted children will do well no matter what and argue that remediation is a better use of funds. This ignores an entire population of students.

Teachers receive little education about the social and emotional needs of gifted students, causing gifted and 2e students to go unrecognized. Before I knew better, I did not understand that some of my underperforming students were actually my most gifted learners, believing poor handwriting or behavior issues were acceptable reasons to question a child's intelligence.

Well-meaning educators say, "All children are gifted." This thinking hinders needed progress, because though all children possess unique gifts, not all children are *born* gifted.

Keep in mind the Columbus Group's definition of giftedness:

[A]synchronous development *in which advanced cognitive abilities and heightened intensity combine to create inner experiences and awareness that are qualitatively different from the norm. This asynchrony increases with higher intellectual capacity. The uniqueness of the gifted renders them particularly vulnerable and requires modifications in parenting, teaching and counseling in order for them to develop optimally.*[3]

Q. What challenges do twice-exceptional kids face?

A. Many, but the lack of understanding and education present the biggest challenge. Parents, educators, physicians, and the child must understand the unique issues that come with being 2e. Twice-exceptional children have been misrepresented as unmotivated, lazy, difficult, disruptive, and more. Out of frustration, the 2e child may claim these descriptors for himself.

Incapacitating perfectionism often plays a role for many 2e children. The 2e learner wants to produce what her intellect allows, but is disappointed when her lack of real skills or experience prevents the product from looking the way she imagined. Her unattainable standards can lead her to question her self-worth.

Parents and teachers can be unaware of the sensory needs of 2e learners. While other students look forward to unstructured times (recess, lunch, PE), a 2e learner may find these torturous. Difficulty with crowds, sounds, or smells can contribute to friendship issues and increase frustration in an already challenging environment.

Many schools find it difficult to meet the social/emotional issues of 2e children. Some do not accept that they have specific needs at all. Instead, these students are more likely to be labeled as behaviorally disordered, oppositional and defiant, emotionally disordered, developmentally delayed, learning disabled, or some combination of these, rather than gifted.[4]

Q. What steps can I take if I realize that my child is 2e?

A. First, *breathe!* Parenting a 2e child is challenging. You might have felt judged and incompetent as a parent. Teachers also feel ineffective when previously successful strategies repeatedly fail.

Second, *change your expectations.* I realized I needed to give up my preconceived ideas of what parenting was *supposed* to be; I was determined to start fresh once I was armed with my new understanding. This is important for educators as well.

Third, *educate yourself.* Find out about 2e children and the specific challenges your child exhibits. That high IQ might be hiding social, motor, or sensory deficits, communication challenges, anxiety, attention or learning difficulties. Find experts and connect with other parents and educators. And read on for information to empower you to lift up and support your 2e children and students.

Believe you can and you're halfway there.

~Theodore Roosevelt

Why is Any of This Important?

Yesterday is not ours to recover, but tomorrow is ours to win or lose.
~Lyndon B. Johnson

We have all heard about the inventors, the artists, and the scientists who have made all-important contributions to our society. Many discoveries came from people who had complicated minds and differences that were not always celebrated.

The passions of our 2e students should be developed into life skills and careers. In reality, however, these students have few opportunities to stretch their thinking and participate in meaningful, active learning in traditional school settings. Gifted children are likely to be the next generation's innovators and leaders—yet the exceptionally smart often remain invisible in the classroom, as they lack the curricula, teacher input, and external motivation to reach their full potential.[1]

Is it Financial?

The word "gifted" turns off many people who view it as elitist or bragging. But ask any parent of a truly gifted child, and you will discover that ensuring a meaningful education and dealing with the unique social and emotional needs is not the easy road many assume.

When school budgets are tight, one of the first academic programs dropped is the gifted and talented support (unless your state has ruled differently). The current emphasis on helping the most struggling students to catch up and work at grade level often leaves the students with the highest IQs to flounder. Boredom and underachievement can result, as well as often ignored complicated social and emotional issues.

Currently Accepted?

Now, take the issues often present in gifted education and multiply those by the added complexities, intensities, sensitivities, and confusion about the twice-exceptional students. Even experienced teachers and principals feel underprepared, leaving parents to tackle these issues with little support from those whom they consider experts.

Educators often view Gifted and Talented (GT) classes as a privilege, not a right. Just when 2e students should be receiving the most understanding, their social, emotional, and learning disabilities are used against them. Some students have had their participation in GT classes taken away due to behavior issues within their regular classroom or even at recess. A lack of social skills can impede the 2e learner when the emphasis is largely on cooperative projects. No one would consider taking away special education services as a punishment.

On more than one occasion, I have tried to educate someone about twice-exceptionality and was met with offhanded comments about the diagnosis. "Does that mean they're twice as smart? If they are so smart, how could school be hard?" This lack of understanding might explain why many classrooms focus on 2e children's behavior problems, instead the support and specific accommodations they require to shine.

Even Good Teachers?

I think about the student who excelled at drawing, only to be told that the schedule does not allow time for art. I think about the boy who wanted to read, but was told to join sharing time despite his obvious discomfort. I think about the girl who needed to move, but instead was told to sit and finish her work, ignoring the fact that she concentrated better on her feet.

I hate to admit that I was the teacher of those students. I did not understand how my "not now" or "when you're finished with your *real* work" comments discredited those students' strengths. I believed I was doing the right thing. I had been taught what listening behaviors looked like and the importance of reinforcing those skills in order to maintain a positive learning environment. Instead of celebrating what was inherently right for these children, I diminished their gifts, which was certainly not my intent when I went into education.

Educators continue to push the needs of their brightest students to the side because of pressure to raise test scores for those students not meeting standard. Classroom teachers may not understand that by not addressing their 2e students' unique strengths and needs, they are actually making their job more challenging.

Twice-exceptional children cannot tolerate boredom or busy work. While no student should be subjected to meaningless busy work, the gifted students' behaviors will often deteriorate and disrupt the classroom environment. When this cycle is repeated, it reinforces the misunderstanding about twice-exceptional students.

What Now?

Many parents are looking for alternatives and some are choosing to take their children out of their neighborhood schools. They look to other possibilities such as private or charter schools, online programs, or homeschooling. Although this saddens me as a public school teacher, as a parent, I understand. I felt that I had no other choice but to look for another option when my relentless advocating did not improve my child's school experience.

We chose homeschooling and can now provide purposeful, hands-on learning, while simultaneously supporting our son's interests and needs. We emphasize increased personal responsibility, problem solving, and building persistence and stamina. We focus on questioning and researching answers, making connections, and leading with interesting, personal topics. We work toward developing a love of learning. This flexible and non-judgmental setting has done wonders for my son and has been proven to help many other 2e children.

I am moved by the emotional stories shared by parents who have switched from traditional school to homeschool. They see immediate changes in their children's attitudes toward learning and about their self-worth. Many say they only regret not leaving their school sooner.

But what about the other gifted and 2e students left in our classrooms? We should understand that those who stay miss social and educational opportunities, especially when much of the focus remains on improving the education of the lowest achieving students.

When I think about my own classroom, when all students feel valued, everyone clearly benefits. Students learn about educational, social, and emotional differences. They develop compassion and empathy. We learn from each other through discussions and active participation. I have watched twice-exceptional students teach their classmates and, in turn, I have witnessed the 2e students gain self-confidence and self-acceptance.

Many successful, creative people share that they did not discover their true passion in school. In fact, school was seen as a road block. As Sir Ken Robinson, PhD, powerfully stated in *The Element*:

> *Some of the most brilliant, creative people I know did not do well at school. Many of them didn't really discover what they could do—and who they really were—until they'd left school and recovered from their education.*[2]

As parents and educators, we are responsible for encouraging curiosity and honoring questioning and divergent thinking. We need to educate children so that they can think beyond themselves and the now. This requires a shift in thinking, but is truly our best chance as a society to succeed.

What is *Boost* ?

Boost is a series of twelve strategies I used when working with my own child and my students to support 2e learners. The strategies are:

Educate
Communicate
Investigate
Separate
Anticipate
Accommodate
Accelerate
Fascinate
Participate
Evaluate
Negotiate
Appreciate

Incorporating all twelve steps when teaching your 2e students will create a positive approach and strengthen outcomes in the learning environment. Whether in a traditional school or homeschool, the twelve steps of *Boost* will change your relationship with your 2e learners and help instill confidence and a love of learning in them.

> *Likewise, as concerned parents as well as citizens, we must seriously examine how effectively our present system of education meets the needs of all students and consider its potential impact on the future of our nation.*
>
> ~*Bright Not Broken*

Boost Strategies

Boost Strategy 1: Educate

Education is not the filling of a pail, but the lighting of a fire.
~William Butler Yeats

In order to educate our twice-exceptional children, their influencing adults must first educate themselves about these children's unique challenges and missed opportunities. Classroom teachers and homeschooling parents should encourage creativity and divergent thinking, promote problem-solving, incorporate children's interests, and consider how learning can develop into lifelong skills for our twice-exceptional students.

Educate Yourself about 2e Learners and Giftedness

A common misconception states that all gifted children are high-achieving, highly motivated leaders, capable of taking an already understood concept and stretching it deeper on their own. I used to think that my gifted students would be my assistants, willing to help struggling classmates understand and finish their work. I judged their benefit to the classroom as more valuable than their sometimes scattered and personal process. This was an unfair assumption.

Twice-exceptional children are often passionate about specific, even archaic, subjects or topics. They desire to learn all that they can, immediately and fully. Once satisfied, they move to another subject. This learning style does not necessarily fit well with the traditional school setting which requires repetition and allows little time for student interests to be explored. The discrepancy creates a dynamic where a student's increased frustration leads to negative behaviors.

Instead of ignoring the way a twice-exceptional student devours topics, teachers can honor this learning style when they provide opportunities to share. After intentionally developing a welcoming classroom culture where students are taught the norms of being an audience member, individuals could sign up for five-minute presentations during a "show and tell" format. In truth, this action honors all students: those who are willing to share and those who help create an environment where sharing is welcomed.

Homeschooling parents and classroom teachers need to remember that new learning should be within the 2e child's ideal range. The learning should be challenging enough, yet attainable to the child. Lessons should be built on his interests and strengths in order to form connections and improve his understanding. Encouraging him to take risks, rewarding his effort, and moving at his pace helps to address the issues of perfectionism—a big issue with this population.

A twice-exceptional child will not, nor should be asked to, tolerate an abundance of wasted time. Do not assign her busy work just to keep her occupied while others catch up. Consider this for all students, though it holds especially true for the 2e learner.

Similarly, many 2e children become frustrated when they must prove their understanding of an already mastered skill. Keep the learning moving for these students so that they can understand the value of the long school day. (See the Boost Strategies "Accommodate" and "Accelerate" for deeper discussions of this issue.) And to help them manage the school day and workload, as with all students, 2e students should be taught time management, study skills, and organizational techniques. How to properly use a planner or homework calendar and keeping an organized desk are skills that should not be assumed because of a student's high IQ. Color-coded folders or pens used for specific subjects, updating a prioritized list of assignments, and labeled folders for completed and unfinished work can be helpful. In addition, a supportive adult should teach the 2e student how to clean and maintain a clutter-free work space.

Twice-exceptional students often struggle with friendship skills and understanding social norms. Remember that, despite the child's intellect, the 2e child may require explicit teaching of strategies to gain and keep friends. Though many families of 2e children stick with traditional school for socialization, most homeschooling parents work on social communication and social norms with their 2e children more deliberately than a teacher with a room full of students can.

I cannot stress enough the importance of a good relationship with your 2e learner. These children are routinely misunderstood, described as disruptive, inflexible, bossy, or unmotivated. A trusting relationship will allow a 2e student to push himself beyond his comfort zone. Teachers must show compassion and interest in his education. This will provide valuable currency for you as you work with your 2e students.

Now, Educate Yourself about This Child

Before you can truly educate a twice-exceptional child, you must consider her as an individual. To do this, consider the following:

- Is she introverted or extroverted?

- What overexcitabilities and sensitivities are present?

- What are her strengths? Her interests? Her worries?

I did not know about Dabrowski's Theory of Overexcitabilities (see page 18) for much of my teaching career. I expected that a gifted child would be bright in all subjects. I questioned giftedness when I noticed substantial peaks and valleys. After educating myself, I understood that the more intense and sensitive a child, the greater the extremes.

Teachers and homeschooling parents should educate a 2e child while nurturing his specific strengths. Successful teachers are open to take what they know about a child's interest and adapt some of the day's lessons. This could include finding books that cover his interests or allowing a self-selected topic for a writing assignment. Addressing a child's learning gaps can be more successful when a portion of his day is spent on his interests, not just consumed by his struggles.

Environment is integral to education, especially for 2e learners. Consider your specific 2e child. Can she can go somewhere to recover, if needed? Do table arrangements have the flexibility to allow for independent work, as well as group work? Is the environment organized with expected places for supplies? Are the walls cluttered?

Some families have found that diet plays an important part in their child's ability to function throughout the day. Food or additive sensitivities or allergies may impact a child's concentration and problem-solving abilities. The sensations of hunger or thirst may be hard for a 2e child to ignore and can distract from his learning. Some children prefer smaller meals and need to eat more frequently than their peers. Parents should consider sharing these specific needs with school personnel, and school personnel should view such requests as beneficial information. (For more information, see "Parent Survey" on page 47.)

Many families learn that counseling, especially with a therapist experienced in gifted or 2e issues, can help with stress management and perfectionism tendencies. Once parents and educators stop focusing on correcting an undesirable behavior and instead recognize the driving force behind a child's actions, learning takes place.

The Impact of Social and Emotional Needs and Educating

Before we can educate 2e children, we must value social and emotional needs as much as intellectual growth. Many power struggles could be avoided if we focused on the 2e child's feelings of self-worth. She is often misunderstood and her giftedness is challenged. It is harder for her to maintain friendships and communicate her feelings. This, along with possible perfectionism, underachievement, and habitual boredom can be damaging.

As part of valuing emotional needs, we should teach kids to recognize when their mind and body are overwhelmed. Teach kids during the calmer times to identify those feelings before they become too big and prevent problem-solving from taking place. Some families and educators have found success with attaching colors or numbers to a continuum of feelings. Yellow might be a warning that assistance could be needed. Perhaps anything over seven on a scale from one to ten might indicate that the twice-exceptional child needs help. It is important for influencing adults to model this with their own feelings and that these colors and numbers are used for educating instead of punishing or shaming.

As part of the process, children should be taught recovery strategies for when a "red time" approaches. Some students find that being allowed to escape the emotionally fueled circumstances is enough. For example, some students might need quiet (e.g., reading, Legos, drawing), while others might need noise (e.g., exercise, jumping, music with headphones) to assist in their recovery. A previously established location, such as a coatroom or right outside the classroom door, could give the student some privacy to pursue her recovery strategy away from the rest of her classmates.

Whatever specific strategies help, allow children to return with grace. It can be helpful for the student and teacher to discuss ahead of time how the student returns to class. After a child returns, avoid immediately discussing what took place. Some teachers find that students prefer to draw or write about their feelings, rather than talking. Through practice and troubleshooting strategies for future incidents, twice-exceptional students will increasingly address their sensitivities in independently.

Ready for Lessons

Once you understand who this twice-exceptional child is, the real educating can begin. Whether you are at home or in a classroom, allowing flexibility with scheduling and providing breaks leads to a more successful day for your 2e student.

Although classroom teachers are typically provided curriculum, they should work to create opportunities where students' interests are explored, such as through reading or self-selected writing topics.

Tweaking math problems or allowing choice for research topics can increase a child's interest and success. Technology, music, and art can add value to the school day for all students.

I am often asked about curricula specifically designed for 2e students. In my opinion, there is no *best* curriculum or program for 2e learners. Regardless of the curriculum, lead with strengths and interests while providing support.

Twice-exceptional children will fail if we fail to educate teachers about their gifts and disabilities. By using the twelve *Boost* strategies, you will work to prevent this from happening on your watch. You can be part of the solution. Parents, be your child's advocate. Teachers, speak to your colleagues and administrators and model what it is like to be a life-long learner. I believe those educators will find this information long overdue.

Develop a passion for learning. If you do, you will never cease to grow.
~Anthony J. D'Angelo

Boost Strategy 2: Communicate

Get in touch with the way the other person feels. Feelings are 55% body language, 38% tone and 7% words.

~Albert Mehrabian

According to the Oxford Learner's Dictionaries, "communicate" means "to exchange information, news, ideas, etc. with somebody." Sounds simple enough, right? Then, why can effective communication be so difficult? As we all have experienced, communication is more than just the words spoken; it is also the nonverbal messages sent. My conversations with parents and educators and my personal experiences indicate that communicating with a twice-exceptional student can be challenging. Less-developed friendship skills, laser-focused interests, and unapproachable body language are just a few of the road blocks people encounter when trying to communicate with 2e kids.

Empathetic speaking and close listening are vital when establishing on-going communication with anyone, but especially for homeschooling parents and classroom teachers with twice-exceptional learners. Because communication skills are not always part of a 2e student's skill set, they must be modeled and practiced.

Consider this common situation: You ask a question that implies choice, such as asking a 2e learner if she would like to read. In actuality, you expect her to read, so she does not truly have a choice. The outcome? A frustrated child who thought she had a choice, and a confused adult who thought the request was clear. To avoid these situations, the adult should work with the child to establish the expectations before reading begins. This models good communication skills and allows the child to practice them.

Nonverbal Confusion

Keep in mind that many twice-exceptional students have difficulty understanding messages when the words and the nonverbal messages do not match. For example, if someone smiles when they sound frustrated, meaning breaks down for some 2e listeners. Another example of mismatched messages is when an adult asks a child to stop moving while the adult continues to walk briskly through the space. A 2e listener may find the difference between the verbal and non-verbal actions confusing. Instead, consider that your body should demonstrate your request. In the case of wanting a child to stop moving, stand in one spot and give the directions before moving again; now, your verbal and non-verbal messages go hand-in-hand.

I have found that visual reminders for directions add clarity to daily lessons. In my classroom, responsibility shifts to the students when I put the visual directions on the board or on sticky notes on their desks. If a student needs redirection, I can point to the nonverbal cues as a guide. I find it helpful to check in with students by asking them to point to where they are in the directions, for example, "If you are on step three, please hold up three fingers."

Homeschooling parents have found similar systems for home responsibilities and daily lessons helpful. A checklist by a child's bedroom door can remind him to make his bed, collect his laundry, and turn out the light before joining the family for breakfast. A list of the daily lessons to be crossed off upon completion can help to develop important time management skills. These lists can be pictures, words, or a combination of both depending on the child's abilities.

The use of visual reminders only works if you desire to help the student, not judge or shame him. Discussing the purpose of your methods prior to implementation will help his understanding. Your facial expression should show caring and empathy, not disappointment, if work remains uncompleted.

Eye Contact

Many 2e children do not make eye contact when they speak with others. Yet, educators often emphasize the importance of eye contact. Students are told "1, 2, 3 eyes on me" or asked to sit in "listening posture" which includes eyes on the speaker. Although not true of all cultures, eye contact is often seen as respect and good manners. I suggest that we question the importance of all students maintaining eye contact. A 2e child's eye contact will likely diminish when meeting new people, feeling reprimanded, or being overwhelmed, and drawing attention to it will only increase the 2e child's discomfort.

Instead of pushing the issue of eye contact, consider other options. Stand side by side with a student to start building communication, or try holding a shared object (a ball, plush toy, etc.) to help maintain contact. Then, have the student repeat the instructions in her own words. These will help create the trust and understanding 2e children need when attempting to share, take risks in a classroom, or engage in discussions with family and friends.

Social Communication

Everyday life is filled with opportunities to work on social communication skills, in and out of the classroom. Twice-exceptional children can practice buying something in a store, ordering at a restaurant, or answering questions from the librarian. Coaching the 2e child for specific situations will increase the likelihood of success.

Many twice-exceptional learners use a literal interpretation of words, leading to misunderstandings. Consequently, keep in mind the effect of tone and intent when teaching and modeling effective communication. For example, if a classroom teacher says "just a minute" in response to a request, the 2e student may expect attention in sixty seconds, which can be misinterpreted as sarcastic. Students will find statements such as "I can help you when I am finished with this student" or "I will answer your question next" clearer. Influencing adults should monitor their own communication style, tone, and word choice to eliminate ambiguity.

Understanding that communication is reciprocal—someone shares and then the other responds with follow-up comments or questions—takes practice. A 2e student may not recognize the social cues, such as those when someone is done listening about her latest fascination. Likewise, when a 2e student is uninterested in a discussion, she may find it hard to be present when the other child shares. This requires purposeful teaching and provides opportunities for role playing. Develop a class culture where social cues are discussed and give students the chance to practice both sides of the situations to see each other's perspective. Many families find it helpful to practice this during meals or when playing games together.

Classroom teachers can teach conversation skills to their whole group during class meetings or with smaller groups as issues arise. Some teachers and 2e students find it helpful to touch base after recess or lunch if ongoing support is needed. I have used pre-established signals (a quick thumbs up or a 1-5 rating with fingers) with students which allow for a quick check-in without drawing attention to the individual student. Some schools also have special education teachers and/or counselors experienced in teaching social skills, who can either work directly with a student or provide guidance to teachers.

Additionally, some 2e students will have experience with Speech and Language Pathologists (SLPs) where social communication is practiced; however, many 2e learners will not qualify for such services. Unfortunately, the focus remains on articulation, while social communication services seem harder to obtain. As a classroom teacher, discuss with your SLP strategies in small group instruction. Consider how you could adjust those lessons to benefit your student.

When Communication Breaks Down

Miscommunication upsets typical students, but even more so the 2e child. Frustration sets in when he struggles to get his thoughts across or does not feel heard. As a result, he might demonstrate his sadness or anger in detrimental ways. From my own experience and in conversations with other parents, this communication breakdown seems to be where many outbursts originate: a lack of communication skills followed by embarrassment.

I remember a particular student who had made quite a name for himself due to loud outbursts. We came up with strategies to help him feel more comfortable and together assigned nonverbal signals (a red cup he placed on his desk was his preferred signal) to alert me when he needed help. For him, a walk around campus made a difference. (Other students find music, sensory bins, or drawing helpful.) Better understanding this student's actions helped us limit future communication breakdowns.

Whether you are a teacher or parent, addressing misunderstandings during the middle of an outburst is ineffective and risks potentially escalating the situation. Wait until everyone is calm and respect the fact that this process might take longer. Once you are both ready, talk through the scenario and work to label the feelings that were part of the situation. Discuss alternative reactions and how new strategies might help. Talk through triggers that may have caused communication breakdown in the first place. Finally, help the 2e child learn to forgive himself and move forward. This, too, requires practice and modeling.

Similarly, feeling overwhelmed and unprepared makes parenting difficult. Children need parents to model problem-solving and communication skills, making self-care critical for parents. Getting plenty of sleep and exercise, as well as taking time to pursue one's own interests, supports parents' emotional health. Reaching out to other parents or supportive family and friends also makes a difference.

Communication Plan

Effective classroom teachers recognize the importance of positive communication with parents, but you will see its value even more so with parents of a 2e child. These parents have likely been on a long and often bumpy journey, and will appreciate the opportunity to share their insights and connect with their child's teacher.

Set up a communication plan early with parents. Decide on the most convenient form of communication—phone calls or emails—and the frequency. Expect more contact in the beginning of the year with reduced communication as the year progresses, adjusting the amount of communication as needed on behalf of the student.

As part of the plan, teachers should assure parents of a balanced perspective. Parents value reports that do not concentrate solely on their child's all-too-familiar struggles. Remember to allow this child the same grace you would any child. For example, if all students were overly excited due to a special activity, the 2e child should not be penalized.

It has been my experience that emails and notes can be misinterpreted. Sometimes a phone call is a better way to share information. If you (parent or teacher) are concerned that your true intent might be lost, take the time to call.

Communication with Other Personnel

Specialists, such as librarians, PE teachers, music teachers, have reported feeling left out of important discussions about their students. While not deliberate, scheduling issues can cause this disconnect. Still, communication with specialists will help lead to the success of 2e students. For example, the echoing of the gym or the loud instruments in music can be challenging for a 2e student with sensory issues. Without the proper information, specialists can unknowingly escalate a situation that otherwise could have been addressed.

Librarians should definitely be informed about your 2e student, as they are in the unique position to support and encourage high interest subjects at appropriate reading levels. Books should not be limited due to students' chronological age or interests of typical classmates. By communicating your 2e student's special needs to the librarian, you will ensure the value of library time and help place the librarian in the role of mentor, something many 2e children crave. Keep in mind that some students do not like to be singled out. Librarians can have pre-selected titles to suggest while other students look for their books.

Parents and educators should also acknowledge the critical role educational assistants (EAs) play. Due to sensory, motor, and social skills, recess and the lunchroom can be troublesome for 2e students. Typically, EAs supervise these times. Many parents feel frustrated when support personnel handle the most stressful parts of their child's day, leading to uninformed discipline decisions. Whether the EAs are staff employees or parent volunteers, they should be educated to support all students. Some schools include EAs in their staff meetings or have made training mandatory before volunteers help in classrooms or playgrounds. If the school does not provide such training, parents can approach the PTA or administrator about the importance of training. When teachers, parents, administrators, and the other adults who are part of the school communicate, all students benefit.

> *Whatever the manifestation, communication impairments often result in sudden, explosive behaviors because of a child's frustration at his inability to communicate effectively with others, to understand their expectations, and to get his needs met.*
> *~Bright Not Broken*

Boost Strategy 3: Investigate

Good questions outrank easy answers.

~Paul Samuelson

When we investigate, we explore. Students learn best when they are interested in the topics of study. Ideally, they should be allowed to investigate without imposed ideas about finished products. Although time constraints add an extra challenge, this process of investigation is imperative for the 2e child. Purposefully using the "Investigate" *Boost* strategy will help classroom teachers, homeschooling families, and parents support their twice-exceptional learners.

Incorporate Investigation

Some of my happiest days as a parent were when I ignored the clock and instead covered my dining table with art supplies for my son to investigate. The purpose was not to finish a planned project, but to allow him time to explore mediums, consider various tools, and discover how much glue could be poured on a piece of paper before it collapsed.

Readers of my blog, MyTwiceBakedPotato.com, and parents with whom I have spoken have found similar results in their own homes. Legos spread across the basement floor, building blocks, ingredients from the pantry, pieces intended for one board game borrowed for an invented game all feed curiosity. Opportunities to investigate go beyond the dining room table into music, mud puddles, insects—endless opportunities abound.

The greatest success happens when investigating takes place free of preconceived ideas or judgment. As the homeschooling parent or classroom teacher, resist tidying up the environment or directing exploration. Nothing stops learning faster and squashes enthusiasm for future investigating than stepping uninvited into a child's investigation.

Understandably, the restrictions of the typical classroom—the number of students, tight curriculum, scheduling, limited supplies—could prohibit the daily freedom to explore. Yet, teachers and parents have seen the benefits of purposefully including these investigations when possible. For example, before embarking on a planned science unit about force and motion, set up a table with collected materials to design and test theories. Allow students time to explore art supplies at a station while other students complete work. Investigation within a classroom setting requires planning and sometimes extra volunteers, but the advantages in making this part of a classroom culture will become readily apparent.

Lead Through Investigation

Twice-exceptional children benefit from witnessing adults question and explore the next steps in their own investigation process. This reinforces that even you do not know all the answers, which can be helpful for those 2e children who struggle with perfectionism.

If you are a homeschooling parent, you can easily incorporate investigation as part of your schooling. Begin with your child's interests and explore her questions and ideas, which in turn will create more questions and learning opportunities.

One of the most beloved places in my classroom has always been the Creation Station. Students are thrilled with the donated paper tubes, yarn, materials, buttons, glitter, and other items that families send to school. I provide tape, staplers, fancy scissors, and hole-punchers, and order student-requested items such as decorative paper or pipe cleaners. The items are in a cupboard that can be closed so that the contents are hidden for most of the day. This is an important part of the Creation Station for both you and students who appreciate an organized environment. Once open, students search for ways to use donated velvet ribbon or stickers to create something pleasing to them. The time and subsequent mess are worth it once you observe a group of kids who would not usually be friends cooperatively drawing plans to make a ramp out of cardboard and duct tape.

Though I do not assess the masterpieces created during this time, the investigation process provides me with insight into all of my students. Seemingly quiet students take on leadership roles and those typically not sought for play are recruited for their known intellectual gifts. A Creation Station can be implemented in any classroom or home. Consider letting friends and family know about your need for leftover crafts materials. You will find them eager to get those items out of their crowded junk drawers.

In addition to hosting a Creation Station for investigation, classroom teachers and homeschooling families can dedicate a shelf where items are left and inspected with a magnifying glass. Shells, nests, rocks, and other finds from nature pique students' curiosity. As students understand that investigation is part of your learning culture, more students will participate and feel safe sharing items.

Physical exploration is only one aspect of investigation. After engaging in conversations with students about their interests, teachers should fill their class library with books based on those topics. Harry Potter, Star Wars, Lego, and nonfiction books about animals or the human body are consistently popular choices. Because 2e learners devour topics quickly, switch books often. Frequent conversations with your 2e students will help you know what subjects they want to investigate next. Perhaps famous artists have captured their attention? Chess? A new author or book series?

As a teacher or homeschooling parent, the word "investigate" should remind us that we are not always seeking mastery or completed research. Remember to ask, "What makes you think that?" or "What's next?" Investigating leads to unplanned, authentic learning.

Investigation Builds Relationships

Investigating alongside a child who has invited you not only improves learning and curiosity for the child, but supports the adult-child relationship. The twice-exceptional child feels honored when those important adults in his life take interest in his investigations. Approaching learning together as equals adds value and purpose to the investigating.

Investigation takes time and active listening. It requires attention to the 2e child's questions or comments. It means following her lead and stopping what you are doing to look up information on the computer or in a book. I carry sticky notes so that I can jot down students' questions or place a note on their desk as a visual reminder to follow up with them. I leave myself notes about books, articles, or sites that drive students' investigations further. Most 2e children want to learn at this increased, deeper pace. Additionally, by encouraging students to participate in the act of investigating, the influencing adults help counteract the issue of perfectionism. Emphasizing the process lessens the need to find the *right* answers, increasing the value of the time spent, while decreasing the pressure to be right or finished.

While investigating engages learning during the day, many 2e children have difficulty calming their minds at night. This seems to be when 2e learners choose to ask deeply thought-out questions. Like using sticky notes in the classroom, some families have found success in writing down questions or ideas in a notebook. This routine may not only help calm your child's mind, but also create a starting point for the next day's investigations.

Investigate the Investigator

Building a respectful relationship benefits all children, but especially your twice-exceptional child. In order to get to know your 2e student, take the time to investigate instead of making quick decisions based on preconceptions. Take on the role of detective and ask your 2e student questions to gain valuable information. Understandably, building a relationship of trust will take time, especially if the student has felt misunderstood by other educators in the past. Because of that, I believe that a great starting point is an interest inventory filled out by the parents, perhaps in conjunction with their child.

~•••~

Parent Survey

1. What are some of your child's interests?
2. What motivates your child?
3. How does your child learn best?
4. What are some specific strengths?
5. What are some challenges?
6. Is your child an extrovert or introvert?
7. Is your child comfortable with compliments?
8. How can I effectively deliver suggestions?
9. Do you have any concerns?
10. Does your child have any concerns?
11. How will I know when your child is overwhelmed? How does your child recover?
12. If nothing seems to be working, what do you try at home?

~•••~

I have seen other interest inventories, but some were not thorough enough to get to the core of what makes a student unique, while others were far too detailed. I believe these questions are specific enough without requiring too much time from busy parents.

As a teacher, I have used my Parent Survey to guide parent conferences and to check in with students during the school year. As a parent, answering these questions provides some peace of mind. You can give your child's teacher critical information without worrying about being viewed as difficult or pushy. Believe me, I have played both roles and completely understand.

Investigate as an Advocate

Many parents have found out the hard way that not all schools are created equal, even when the school claims to be specifically geared for gifted students. If you are a parent looking for a better fit in a new school, ask about the school's culture and the staff's understanding of giftedness and 2e learners. How are 2e learners served? What accommodations are made? Do the administration and teachers understand the complex social and emotional issues that often accompany twice-exceptional learners?

In addition to asking these questions of the educators in charge, parents can deepen their investigation by seeking out families who currently attend the school. They might be willing to share their own experiences and provide inquiring parents with another perspective.

The same advice holds for homeschooling families looking at outside learning opportunities. While some groups or classes describe themselves as "enrichment" for gifted students, if they are not familiar with 2e learners, they can be a waste of time and money. In addition, a poor experience can discourage the 2e child from trying future classes. Ask about the number of students in the class, if students can move at their own pace, and how knowledgeable the teachers are in the subject. Personal experience and stories from my readers have proven that investigating a class or school ahead of time can prevent challenging situations later.

Dare to ask questions and seek answers to the puzzles of life.
~Lailah Gifty Akita

Boost Strategy 4: Separate

Our prime purpose in this life is to help others. And if you can't help them, at least don't hurt them.

~Dalai Lama

The *Boost* strategy of "Separate" plays out in several contexts:

- Educators need to separate themselves from challenges they might have experienced with previous gifted or twice-exceptional students.

- School personnel must separate their previous ideas about what it means to be gifted and twice-exceptional from the realities of true giftedness.

- All influencing adults need to separate the 2e child from the struggles they encounter.

While giftedness and twice-exceptionality share attributes, the 2e child is often more misunderstood, more intense, and more mislabeled. Unfortunately, many educators do not understand that a child can be simultaneously gifted and disabled. As the new teacher in your 2e student's life, encourage her to see you and the new classroom as a new experience, separate from past teachers who did not understand her.

When the influencing adults in a twice-exceptional child's life practice "Separate," it benefits not only the 2e child but also the parents, the teacher, and other students in that learning environment.

How to Separate from the Past

Children deserve a fresh start when the new school year begins. Of course, many factors contribute to a challenging year, including the teacher, class makeup, schedule, and curriculum. A resourceful teacher will consider the previous year but be ready to move forward with new strategies and accommodations, while taking the time to form her own opinion and relationship with students. Separate your past experiences with previous students who were highly gifted from this current twice-exceptional student. As the saying in 2e circles goes, "If you've met one 2e child, you've met one 2e child." Avoid letting past experiences cloud future relationships. Keep in mind that you now know more than you did before. Greet that child with a genuine smile which will reassure him that you have moved on and that the focus is on the new day.

Considering the challenges many 2e students face, they should have the opportunity to separate the morning's difficulties from the afternoon's possibilities, breaking the day into smaller increments and considering the outcome of each time period. The point is to move throughout the day without grudges or the expectation of failure. This does not mean that we ignore challenges, but instead we work to gather information and help the 2e student use new strategies and accommodations throughout the day.

Sharing inner dialogues and modeling your own ability to move past unforeseen challenges helps 2e children learn to separate their initial emotional reaction from a frustrating experience. For example, "I am disappointed because I wanted to do this art lesson today. Unfortunately, I did not get the right glue. I feel frustrated. I could ask another teacher if they have the right kind or I can stop by the craft store after school and we can do it tomorrow." Twice-exceptional children need to witness problem-solving steps to remind them that everyone tackles problems—that the important part is finding a solution and moving beyond—which addresses both the issues of perfectionism and poor self-esteem common in the 2e population.

Separate the Child from the Struggles

One of the most frequent conversations I have with parents is about their twice-exceptional child being labeled "The Behavior Kid" or "The Tough Kid." Families relate situations where they felt their child was unfairly targeted as a bully or as having caused other problems. Educating educational professionals about twice-exceptionality can help prevent such misunderstandings from negatively impacting our 2e students.

Separate a child's ability to succeed in the classroom from her struggles in other areas, such as music, PE, or recess. A 2e learner who becomes overwhelmed in non-classroom environments should be provided accommodations so she can be ready for learning once she returns to class. Address such difficulties so that heightened emotions and sensory overload do not tarnish the rest of her day.

Additionally, the 2e child must be allowed to return gracefully without the expectation of immediately addressing the situation. Any conversation about his struggle should be done after a calming down period so problem-solving can take place. These conversations should be as private as possible. When teachers make the effort to talk privately and respectfully, all students sense that their feelings will be honored. Use the Parent Survey from the "Investigate" section to learn how to best approach your students so that recovery can take place.

Most parents have witnessed outbursts brought on by hunger, tiredness, inflexibility, or communication challenges. Without meaning to, parents can escalate these episodes by trying to reason with their child in the heat of the moment. Before I knew better, I added fuel to heated situations. When I placed importance on uncovering the reasons for my son's outbursts, they shortened in time and frequency. In addition, our relationship improved once I used fewer words in the moment, allowed him time to recover, and used a situation as a teaching tool instead of considering it a tantrum.

Teachers should learn from parents' experiences and separate a student's hunger, tiredness, and difficulty with transitions from subsequent emotional outbursts. Again, the Parent Survey can help with this. Look for patterns and solutions to help the student. For example, some students are overwhelmed by the noises and smells of the cafeteria. As a result, those students may not eat enough lunch to get through the rest of the day. Consider a short break time where students are allowed to finish their lunch or have a snack.

On those hard days, parents can project their own fears about the future and ignore progress made from increased skills, learned strategies, or maturity. Separate these worries from your child. Separate yourself from the judgment and questions you might feel from family and friends about homeschooling or other parenting choices. Do not let others who have not parented your unique child steer you from your path.

Separate Home from School

Many parents speak about their frustration when teachers seem unable to separate their child from his mistakes. Daily emails or phone calls that rehash ongoing struggles may prove detrimental to the child and certainly disheartening for parents. Setting up an effective communication plan between parents and the teachers will alleviate this negative feedback. All parties should agree on what is valuable information, when contact should be made, and how messages should include successes, as well as challenges. (Refer to the *Boost* strategy "Communication.")

Even if your 2e child attends school without behavior incidents, he will likely be spent once he returns home. Consider his afterschool responsibilities and if they are reasonable. After all, are you eager for additional errands at the end of your long work day?

Conversely, consider separating school from home. Although this may not be a popular opinion with everyone, I do not believe in punishing a child at home for an incident in school. Most likely, he has already received a consequence for the infraction at school. Should he be punished twice, especially when families may not have all the information leading up to the incident? If that approach feels uncomfortable, make a point to hear about the situation from your child's perspective before deciding on a consequence. Use the incident as a teaching tool, talk through the scenario together, and brainstorm more positive reactions. By approaching the situation in this fashion, parents can help the 2e student identify triggers to avoid future incidents.

After trying all these, if you still witness your child's self-worth suffering and continued anxiety about school, recognize that something needs to change. Accommodations might make a difference or time spent with qualified professionals could help; however, it may be time to blend home and school together and start homeschooling where "separate" is no longer as important. A social structure like a school, which values order and cooperation, may not fit a divergent thinker or a child with a slow or fast tempo, as those traits make order and cooperation more difficult.[1]

Reframing

One of the most effective things you can do to separate your child from unflattering characteristics is to "reframe." Reframing means using positive words to describe a concept that typically has a negative connotation.[2] For example, instead of thinking about a child as "stubborn," consider that child as "determined" or "persistent." A student perceived as "bossy" could be characterized as "confident." If our desired outcome is to lift up and support 2e children, then we need to rename the most prevalent characteristics and consider them strengths to celebrate. For example:

Instead of	Consider
Argumentative	Passionate
Hyper	Energetic
Fearful	Cautious

Although I had practiced the technique of reframing, I was unfamiliar with this specific term until I read *When The Labels Don't Fit*, by Barbara Probst. Reframing certainly influences my thoughts as an educator and also allows a new focus for my parenting. It does require practice and commitment, so that parents and educators can access their skills of reframing on the days when emotions run high and patience is limited.

> *Live out of your imagination, not your history.*
>
> ~Stephen Covey

Boost Strategy 5: Anticipate

Think twice before you speak, because your words and influence will plant the seed of either success or failure in the mind of another.

~Napoleon Hill

Through experience and maturity, parents and teachers can anticipate possible consequences. For example, when a teacher witnesses a child leaning back in his chair, that educator will easily anticipate the likely outcome of the child falling to the floor. When a parent sees his child taking food out of a pet's dish, he understands the distinct possibility that the pet will snap or growl at the child.

When you are the parent or teacher of a twice-exceptional child, you tend to spend much of your energy trying to anticipate "what will happen next" and determining if it can be altered for a better outcome. By integrating the *Boost* strategy of "Anticipate," the job can be less daunting and your decisions more effective.

Anticipate Possible Needs Challenges

Past experiences help us anticipate possible future scenarios. Many challenging situations begin when a 2e child inadequately anticipates the effects of a change centered on sensory or basic needs. For example, a 2e child may worry what to do if:

- Snack or lunch is delayed

- She needs to use the restroom during a presentation

- The classroom is too loud

- The desks are moved

- Another class of students joins your class

- She needs help: does she come to you or raise her hand

Educators should remember that even when adjusting the daily schedule for something of high interest to most students, such as a visiting art teacher or a science demonstration, anticipate that changes to the typical schedule could raise some of the students' anxiety levels. Many students, but especially your 2e learners, feel most comfortable when given enough information prior to the event to anticipate how those changes will affect them. For example, if a 2e student struggles with loud noises, his teacher should anticipate that next week's assembly in the gym might be a problem. As part of the expected communication between teacher and parents, the teacher should contact parents ahead of time and discuss possible solutions, such as noise-cancelling headphones or an alternative place for him to stay during the loudest parts of the assembly.

Other challenges to anticipate include:

- **Halloween costumes and decorations:** Consider permitting costumes throughout the day, not just during the scheduled party time. Reassure students that costumes are optional.

- **The first Monday after Winter or Spring Break:** Plan for a less rigorous schedule on the first day back after a long break.

- **Music in the lunchroom:** Create a quiet space where students can escape the over-stimulation (or if they simply don't care for the music).

- **Special events, such as "Backwards Day":** Reassure students that participation is optional.

- **Packing up the classroom on the last days of school:** Depending on their abilities and preferences, either include students in the packing up or minimize their participation.

Without meaning to, schools sometimes sabotage the most vulnerable students in the name of fun for the larger group. Instead, we should anticipate that the emotions of our most sensitive kids will change when the influencing adults suddenly change their expectations. Students and families should be given time for troubleshooting.

Furthermore, a change in weather, a full moon, time changes, or growth spurts can lead to changes in sleep patterns and intensified emotions which parents and teachers need to anticipate. While we cannot control these triggers, they can explain unwanted behaviors, and we can be prepared for more understanding during these times.

Anticipating and having the flexibility to address these issues is certainly an attractive part of homeschooling for many students and families. Teachers should try to anticipate these needs, as well, to keep their 2e learners comfortable and focused on learning.

Anticipate Social Anxiety

Most parents and teachers of twice-exceptional learners have witnessed social anxiety negatively impacting a 2e child's day. Though attending a birthday party, going to a family celebration, or trying an afterschool club may sound like fun for many people, they may prove too much for the 2e child. Sometimes, something as mundane as a family dinner or a visit to the neighborhood park will cause just as much social anxiety as an unknown situation. Guests or outside adults may be confused by this discomfort, especially if they do not have experience with children who have social anxiety.

Social anxiety, though not unique to 2e children, can be exacerbated by their sensitive nature and confusion about their own giftedness and struggles. Sharing as much information as possible with the 2e child ahead of time may alleviate fears, though it may also increase them. As parents of 2e children will tell you, it is a balancing act. Classroom teachers should seek input from parents, since they know their children best. Over time and with the support of parents, teachers will discover what works best.

Anticipate Perfectionism

Just as social anxiety is not unique to 2e children, neither is perfectionism; however, it must be anticipated with 2e children. Gifted children set standards according to their mental, not chronological, age. A nine-year-old mind may make promises that six-year-old hands cannot keep.[1] This asynchronous development leads to feelings of frustration when, despite hard work and strong intellectual understanding, a final project is less than perfect.

Influencing adults in the 2e child's life can fight against perfectionism by encouraging unique responses through writing, art, and music. Focusing attention on the process instead of a finished product celebrates divergent thinking along the way. Mistakes should be considered as opportunities for learning, another chance to try a different strategy.

Stopping a Preferred Activity for a Chore

Imagine the following: Your child does not want to leave the playground for his dentist appointment or perhaps he refuses to stop his video game because he has reached his farthest level and putting on his shoes would "kill" his character. Leaving that entertaining play date at the park or letting his video game character die in order to do an undesirable chore is not easy. To avoid outbursts, parents and teachers must help with transitions from fun activities to chores. Begin with plenty of empathy, both for the likely frustration that will occur when you announce that the fun is over and for the tiresome recovery that will need to take place. Parents should consider this when scheduling the day and anticipate what adjustments will help smooth the transition. Can the child have a five-minute warning at the park? Must the child put on his shoes at that particular moment? If parents expect their children to demonstrate flexibility, they should model the same willingness to be flexible.

When I control the schedule, I take care of the less preferred activity before beginning the engaging activity. If that is not possible, I provide reminders about the time remaining for video games and remind my child about what needs to happen to prepare for the dentist or shopping. Some parents find that warnings given too early can raise the anxiety level. Know your 2e child.

Having flexibility within the daily schedule can be hard for a classroom teacher. She must take into account her specialist schedule, recess, lunch, and required teaching before trying to arrive at the best schedule possible. Each year, teachers attempt to design a daily schedule that will encompass the many teaching demands and accommodate their students' needs. Some educators find that one class handles math better after lunch while a previous class preferred it first thing in the morning. The 2e students in a classroom often need additional transition time built into the schedule. Teachers have found success with visual timers, more frequent transition warnings, and previously discussed agreements about the possibility of being allowed to return to a preferred activity after a required lesson is completed.

Many people find transitioning from fun to chores hard, though practice and maturity helps improve the process. Remember to celebrate any success or improvements.

When You Can't Anticipate the Unexpected

Anticipating requires planning and preparing, but what happens when a situation arises which could not be anticipated such as a surprise fire drill at school or a play date being cancelled due to illness? In these situations, only the increased possibility of heightened emotions can be anticipated.

Because we cannot control everything, incorporate deliberate coaching about being more flexible to the unknown. This takes time, but practicing ahead of time is a must. Parents and teachers can help to label those feelings and model their own feelings when something unexpected takes place. Some have found success using visual aids, such as picture cards showing how a child's face might look when frustrated, disappointed, or angry. Others have used photographs (taken with the child's and parent's knowledge and permission) of the child in the midst of these emotions. Intentionally sharing your inner dialogue with children provides another way of labeling feelings.

We can never plan for all situations. We can, however, anticipate possible solutions for potentially challenging circumstances. Taking the time to prepare our 2e students can lead to more successful coping when the unexpected occurs.

Now, Ignore My Words

For just a moment, I want you to forget my advice from earlier in this chapter. I would like you to consider the value in *not* anticipating.

Allowing learning opportunities to take shape organically is powerful. Stopping by the park unexpectedly or visiting a new bookstore that you stumble across is beautiful. For some of us, myself included, when we get a list of rules, we tend to forget the importance of flexibility, but these unexpected moments can provide pleasure and wonderful memories. Regardless, anticipate success and expect valuable learning to take place.

Keep your face to the sunshine and you cannot see a shadow.

~Helen Keller

Boost Strategy 6: Accommodate

The biggest mistake we make in life is to treat everyone equally when it comes to learning.

~Mel Levine

For many educators and parents, just hearing the word "accommodate" during conferences, doctor's appointments, IEP meetings, or requests for team support meetings causes anxiety. Educators may interpret "accommodate" to mean more work in overcrowded classrooms. Many parents have reported pushback from school personnel about accommodations not specifically protected by an IEP (Individualized Education Plan, designed to meet a child's specific needs) or 504 plan (a plan which outlines accommodations meant to "level the playing field" for students who might not qualify for an IEP), and sometimes even with these plans in place. Occasionally, accommodations are implemented, but not fully, leading to frustrated parents and underserved students. Any child who needs more or less of something—or something different altogether—should not be considered a burden. This negative mindset feeds into an environment where learning cannot take place.

Embrace Needed Accommodations

Twice-exceptional learners face challenges in large part due to the confusion and lack of understanding among teachers, administrators, and parents about what 2e actually means. Until educational professionals are themselves educated about the needs, intensities, sensitivities, and complexities that accompany twice-exceptionality, many 2e learners will continue to be left behind. Simply put, if these students are not considered for accommodations, they will not receive what they need and deserve. By following the *Boost* strategies of "Educate" and "Investigate," you have already begun to understand the reasons for the *Boost* strategy "Accommodate."

A disservice takes place when evaluation scores are combined in order to come to a decision about qualification. Once educators understand the asynchronous development of the 2e learner, they see how this keeps 2e students from receiving the help they need. The highs cancel the lows or the lows hide in the highs. A highly gifted student completing work at grade-level standards is not working to her potential and might still need accommodations in order to even out the discrepancy between her current work and actual ability.

Effective teachers understand that different kids need different things. Even those without IEPs and 504s should have access to strategies and supports to improve their learning. No punishment should be given for the need to accommodate. No obvious, or even subtle, resentfulness should be displayed by the influencing adults. An obsession with everyone doing the same thing leads to inequality for students who have different needs from the norm.[1]

Types of Accommodations

Various accommodations may be necessary for 2e children. Besides academics, assistance with social and emotional growth, sensory processing, and/or motor skills may require accommodations. In fact, one of the accommodations that I encourage parents to seek is the protection of recess. Twice-exceptional students must be allowed recess even when their work is incomplete or their in-class behavior has been challenging. Not only does the social interaction benefit the 2e child, but he must have the opportunity to move his body and escape the classroom environment. Also, students must have their basic needs met before learning can take place, especially 2e students who feel things more intensely than others. Make food and bathroom breaks available, as thinking will come to a halt if the 2e child's body is uncomfortable and he is not allowed to meet those needs.

When building class lists, school personnel should consider more than numbers. Take into consideration individual teachers' strengths. Educators who know the importance of a strong student/teacher relationship, welcome flexibility as to how students demonstrate understanding, and appreciate the unique needs of gifted children will provide a better environment for the 2e student.

Academic Accommodations

Not all students demonstrate knowledge the same way. Especially with your 2e students, allow them to share their learning through alternative projects. Your flexibility permits her to share her strengths without her delays hampering her efforts. Once she meets the given standards, she can move on to a more sophisticated interest.

Writing often presents a challenge for 2e learners due to asynchronous development, motor issues, lack of organization, or possible anxiety and perfectionism. Proven technical accommodations, such as laptops, spell check, or tape recorders, allow complicated ideas to be freed from his mind without the hindrance of getting stuck in the details. Consider these tools even when an IEP or 504 plan is not mandated. Perhaps an assistant could write the student's ideas? Could the student share answers orally or use an app with voice recognition to record his thoughts? How about decreasing the amount of writing to an amount which would still demonstrate mastery, yet not overwhelm the student? Educators have adjusted lessons so that answers can be underlined or circled instead of rewriting the complete thought. Creative teachers use accommodations so that the act of writing does not diminish the student's ability to demonstrate how much he knows.

Math often also requires accommodations, due to the writing component and the sometimes repetitious nature of worksheets. For example, if mastery can be demonstrated with five problems, are twenty necessary? Can a calculator be used to help with the problem-solving and math communication assignments? Perhaps using graph paper instead of lined paper or worksheets will help the student keep track of her numbers?

Depending on the school, the provided pull-out program for gifted and talented students (GATE, G&T, etc.) may not be a good fit for your 2e child. If this is the case, accommodations should be made for the 2e learner to be grouped with intellectual peers regardless of chronological age. The purposeful grouping of afterschool clubs designed around high interest activities such as chess or computer coding have shown success. Some schools have embraced optional book study groups or discussion groups for Minecraft enthusiasts held during recess. Younger students may benefit from spending time in older classes for specific subjects. The goal should be to make accommodations for the 2e student to learn and interact with like-minded students whenever possible.

Environmental Accommodations

Environmental accommodations can provide comfort to the 2e student and should be considered when possible, even if not mandated by an IEP or 504 plan. If the environment is not a good fit, the 2e child will always feel overwhelmed. That is why problems arise for many sensitive and intense children when they start school: prior to that, they had managed because the flexibility of the home environment. Typically, students do not have much flexibility when it comes to the classroom environment. They cannot change the lighting, the temperature, or the hum of the heater. Because of this, educators should be willing to make accommodations when requested and as possible. Are the blinds adjustable? Is the temperature controlled in the classroom? Can desks be moved away from the windows?

Consider your daily schedule and classroom. Do you allow time for students to move? Is there a mix of group seating and individual seats? Can children move if they are distracted at their table group? What about the noise level? When it is loud, can noise-sensitive kids escape from the hubbub? Many environmental accommodations can help a student with sensory issues maintain focus. Some students find success with noise-cancelling headphones. Others prefer standing next to their desk or sitting on a large ball instead of a typical student chair. Fidget toys, molding putty, and chew bracelets are just a few of the many products available. Talk to occupational therapists and special education teachers to learn more.

Regardless of the accommodations, any assessment to evaluate their effectiveness should wait until the accommodations are in place and fully functioning. Teachers and parents should continue to be flexible as accommodations are reviewed and adapted.

Homeschooling Accommodations

While all parents have practice providing accommodations to some extent for their children, parents of 2e children must often provide more accommodations, which makes homeschooling a good option.

Homeschooling looks different in every home. Each family accommodates for their own children when it comes to the teaching schedule, school start and end times, and curriculum. They accommodate for family trips, music lessons, or time with professionals, such as occupational therapists or tutors. If a family had a challenging weekend, Monday can be used to regroup, temporarily pushing aside academics while emotional needs take priority.

Homeschool students are not forced to wait for other students to catch up. Homeschool parents can accommodate for the highs and lows, and do so naturally. Carefully scheduling lessons with breaks in between or spending time on a favored subject are some daily accommodations.

Just like a student in a typical classroom, a homeschool student must have his basic needs met before he can learn effectively. If homeschooling takes the family away from home, as it often does, parents can bring snacks for the day. All parents want their children to feel comfortable, so 2e parents buy tagless garments, adjust home lighting or room temperature, and/or adapt school hours to match with the 2e child's sleep needs. Sensory products used in the classroom might be necessary accommodations for homeschooling students. Doing this at home takes away any possible concern on the child's part that others are watching.

> *Not every child has an equal talent or an equal ability or an equal motivation, but children have the equal right to develop their talent, their ability, and their motivations.*
>
> ~John F. Kennedy

Boost Strategy 7: Accelerate

Start by doing what's necessary; then do what's possible; and suddenly you are doing the impossible.

~Francis of Assisi

"Accelerate," the seventh *Boost* strategy, refers to lessons, homework, and grade or subject acceleration. Twice-exceptional students are often forced to wait for others to understand concepts that they have already mastered. Without the intentional use of acceleration, our brightest minds will not experience the value of learning.

Pacing

Today's educators face an interesting challenge: be flexible and efficient enough with their instructional pacing so that they support their struggling learners, while maintaining the interest of their most talented students. True, most students need some amount of repetition, but gifted students often need little or no repetition, frequently grasping the concept before the teacher's instruction ever begins.

Talented teachers learn that much of their delivery should take place in smaller groups of students with like abilities. This allows for some individuals to be re-taught skills while, ideally, other students move to the next steps or more advanced material. Unfortunately, some educators admit that, despite good intentions, much of their time is consumed by struggling students.

In order to support gifted and 2e students, try not only a quicker pace, but administer pretests to see if the concept needs to be taught at all. While this might seem like more work, consider the payoff: more engaged and less frustrated twice-exceptional learners, as well as more productive classroom time for all students.

Homeschooling families must also consider acceleration. Although most homeschooling families have flexibility with their lessons and pacing, when choosing an online school or enrollment in a district homeschooling program, the pacing can still be out of sync with their gifted child. The amount of repetition and slower approach remains a concern even when the 2e child is in the comfort of his own home. Consequently, some homeschooling families opt out of online programs and instead design a curriculum to suit their individual child—one of the benefits of leaving the brick-and-mortar school.

Compacting

Curriculum compacting is:

> *[A]n instructional technique that allows teachers to adjust curriculum for students by determining which students already have mastered most or all of the learning outcomes and providing replacement instruction or activities that enable a more challenging and productive use of the students' time.*[1]

If a student shows mastery before his classmates, allow him to move to deeper learning. This compacting process should result in the twice-exceptional child engaged in interest-driven, question-seeking, thought-provoking inquiry that proves the value in learning, whether at home or in the classroom.

Homework

The debate about homework has gone on for decades. People disagree not only about the value of homework, but about whether students are assigned too much or too little.[2]

A twice-exceptional student can struggle with homework just like his classmates, sometimes experiencing greater frustration after a long day in an environment that does not match his sensory, social, or academic needs.

Similarly, the 2e child can be confused about his level of frustration with homework. He does not understand why he finds it challenging, when everyone in class brought it home with the expectation that they could do it. This confusion leads to the 2e child to doubt his giftedness, feeding into his perfectionist tendencies, leaving him to worry if he is possibly not as smart as everyone thinks he is and that his parents, teacher, and others might find out "the truth."

He might struggle with his ability to communicate his frustration for completing more of the same work that he has mastered. Perhaps he feels spent from the interaction and sensory overload from the long day. Because twice-exceptional children struggle with perfectionism, the 2e student likely puts increased, and often unreasonable, expectations on himself.

The absence of homework is a clear advantage to homeschooling. If purposeful learning has taken place during the day, will additional practice prove more valuable than time with family or other interests? Some argue that homework builds character and reinforces personal responsibility; however, homeschooling families address those issues without the addition of homework.

If not homeschooling, parents should seek advice from classroom teachers. Many teachers are unaware of the stress homework causes. Perhaps a suggested time limit for assignments can be established, stopping homework at this point whether completed or not. Consider alternative accommodations, such as showing mastery in another way or adding adjustments to an existing 504 plan.

Grade Level

Even more so than homework, grade promotion leads to heated debate among educators and parents. Many schools and districts have policies that discourage children from moving to higher grade levels, citing social concerns and emotional readiness as the biggest reasons against making the change. Others see grade promotion as a possible solution for those students needing accelerated work and challenges to avoid ongoing boredom in their classroom. Many parents and teachers have noticed that once a 2e child is challenged appropriately, much of her anxiety and behavioral concerns diminish.

Grade promotion is not the only option when parents or educators consider acceleration. Subject acceleration, which addresses more specific abilities than the generalized grade level acceleration, can be a successful practice. Remember that many 2e students develop asynchronously. Subject acceleration allows these students to move into a higher grade level for a particular subject, while remaining at grade level for other subjects.

Again the flexibility of homeschooling naturally addresses both subject and grade acceleration. Homeschooling children often read books written for much older students, or pursue math or science at a much higher grade level than their age-mates. By decreasing the time spent on subjects students already know or find less interesting, while increasing the focus on high-interest subjects, homeschooling families innately use acceleration in their learning environment.

Not Everything is Accelerated

The 2e learner may seek academic acceleration through a desire for an increased learning pace and a deeper understanding about the world around them. Meanwhile, their asynchronous development may still necessitate support and accommodation in some subjects or daily tasks. Homeschooled 2e children's daily rituals inherently accelerate some areas while slowing down others. Educators and administrators should consider implementing a similar approach as they support students with varying skills.

In fact, many 2e children require "deceleration," instead of acceleration, in seemingly innocuous areas of the school day. For example, 2e children may find transitions between activities overwhelming, so decelerating transitions may help 2e students focus better on the next activity, helping all students to participate. Parents and teachers need to reassess their expectations of students' social and emotional maturity, and adjust accordingly. Misguided educators have accelerated their expectations of 2e students, assuming that they are capable of independently stretching a mundane lesson until it is meaningful. This type of thinking unfairly sets up the twice-exceptional child to fail, instead of providing him the support necessary for him to succeed.

The 2e child paints a confusing picture for many. On one hand, she appears more advanced with her strong vocabulary and her desire for learning at an accelerated rate, while on the other, she is hampered by her own accelerated expectations and the misguided expectations of those meant to empower her. If allowed to continue, this imbalance will prevent the twice-exceptional child from gaining skills in a positive learning environment.

> *Birth dates help administrators keep track of children, but they don't provide too much information about the needs of the highly gifted.*
>
> *~Genius Denied*

Boost Strategy 8: Fascinate

Wisdom begins in wonder.

~Socrates

When twice-exceptional children attend traditional schools, they often find the already-known curriculum boring, the sensory input around them overpowering, their learning disabilities distressing, and the many social norms and complicated friendship issues frustrating. Those around them often misunderstand and mislabel their behaviors as negative. No wonder 2e children find traditional school an uninviting learning experience.

When teachers and homeschooling families implement "Fascinate" as a *Boost* strategy to support 2e children, they actively work to stretch beyond a child's current interests and identified strengths. The influencing adults strive to fascinate with possibilities and ideas that the 2e student has yet to even consider.

Why Fascinate?

Talented educators understand the importance of keeping twice-exceptional students engaged by making classroom time valuable. In addition to educating himself about twice-exceptional children, providing appropriate accommodations, and accelerating the curriculum whenever possible, the classroom teacher can pique the 2e child's interest by introducing her to a new idea or an extension to one of her already known interests. With minimal planning, a teacher can hand a student a book or pull her aside to see a quick YouTube video, providing added support for a twice-exceptional student's needs.

In most situations, students are placed in classrooms based on their birthdates, not their interests or their skills. Schools should consider finding ways of grouping students with similar interests, increasing the possibility of a teacher purposefully using the "Fascinate" strategy. If teachers considered their students' interests as valuable placement information for the following school year, they could group students interested in chess or other strategy games, talented writers who want to try their hand at poetry, or those who want to stretch their understanding about particular math or scientific concepts. Parents could offer their input about interests they witness at home (another use of the Parent Survey).

Often, I call small groups back to my desk to share something— maybe a book, a photograph, a picture, or a question that I pose just to their group—with the hope of fascinating them. Not only does this typically interest the individual students, but it creates a connection with the other students in the group. Connecting with people who share the same passions affirms that you are not alone, that there are others like you and that, while many might not understand your passions, some passionately share them.[1]

When and How to Fascinate

Until you know each student as an individual, you cannot be prepared to keep them engaged at school. Review the completed interest inventories and consider your impressions from initial conversations. Only after this will you understand how each student learns and what problems might occur if the student feels pushed beyond his comfort level. "Fascinate" can turn into "frustrate" for the student if the teacher falls short with missed opportunities.

An effective strategy for both parents and educators to perfect in terms of "fascinate" is the quick "fly-by" technique. When a student is working on a non-preferred activity or is approaching frustration, lean in and deliver your fascinate statement. A few examples to consider:

- "I know you are interested in physics, I have an app I would like to show you when you are finished."

- "Did you know that JK Rowling wrote another book? Come see me when you are ready and we can look it up together."

- "I heard you say that you were interested in drawing. Have you considered trying animation?"

At first glance, this fly-by might be seen as a distraction that makes completing the undesirable assignment that much harder. My experience has been that reminding the 2e student about other opportunities more geared to her liking and interests serves as a motivator. I use this approach as both a homeschooling parent and a classroom teacher when I need to change the mood or anxiety level of a possibly challenging moment. A fly-by also helps deliver information to fascinate your twice-exceptional child if he is sensitive to being different from the others or is highly-introverted. When timed perfectly, it provides just the *Boost* your 2e student needs.

As the teacher or homeschooling parent, be flexible in your own schedule to allow the fascination to go farther than you planned. Undoubtedly, the most important aspect of the 2e profile is the student's exceptional abilities and areas of interest.[2] Use this to motivate and educate your twice-exceptional children.

Implementing Fascination into Homeschooling

Of course, parents have an advantage as they consider fascination because of their established relationship with their child. Very likely they are already aware of their child's high interest topics and know what will pique their child's curiosity.

Although homeschooling allows for the focus on individual needs, the inclusion of "fascinate" into homeschooling should not be assumed, but purposely included into the schedule and connected to each student. As with classroom educators, scheduling can place restrictions and parents may be tempted to address required lessons before allowing for fascination. Do not dismiss its value.

Fascination is personal. Many times, siblings will not be interested in the same topics. Because of this, parents must have discussions with individual children to gain insight. Ask questions to test interest levels. Consider news, documentaries, and videos to gauge and create interests. Visit libraries, museums, parks, or new restaurants. Connect with groups or clubs dedicated to unique interests. Find mentors. Search for opportunities to fascinate your unique 2e child that will help her appreciate the benefits of learning.

Activities we love fill us with energy even when we are physically exhausted. Activities we don't like can drain us in minutes.

~Sir Ken Robinson

Boost Strategy 9: Participate

Coming together is a beginning; keeping together is progress; working together is success.

~Henry Ford

Implementing "Participate" as a *Boost* strategy to support 2e children is best achieved when all parties in the 2e child's education, including parents, classroom teachers, special education teachers, and the twice-exceptional learner are involved. Educating a 2e child can be overwhelming at times. Only when everyone involved understands the traits of twice-exceptional students will those students receive the education they deserve.

Academic Participation

Twice-exceptional children need to learn what academic participation does and does not look like. Set clear expectations. For example, share scoring rubrics with students and examples of student work which clearly represent each grade so that students can characterize what demonstrates satisfactory work. Homeschooling families typically have more flexibility. Consider having your child help determine the information required for a satisfactory score and discuss which gaps or errors might suggest additional practice.

Keep in mind that many twice-exceptional children are literal and take the rules and expectations at face value and quite seriously. Good communication and a positive relationship between teacher or parent and student play into this dynamic. If the relationship has suffered from past misunderstandings, the adult should work to repair it. (See "Communicate" and "Separate.")

Twice-exceptional children's inquisitive natures often exacerbate their challenges with organization, time management, or other issues that impede their learning. No matter how high the child's IQ, 2e students need to learn strategies to allow them to make connections, organize their ideas, and stay focused. Students have found visual timers, graphic organizers, and an ongoing list (either written on paper or a personal white board) helpful after receiving instruction.

Homeschooling families and classroom teachers should consider appropriate accommodations to maintain participation instead of allowing the 2e child to feel defeated by his disabilities. Depending on the interest level in the subject, stamina and perseverance may also be factors. It is not uncommon for teachers and families to observe a 2e student who reads about chemistry for forty minutes, but cannot tolerate ten minutes of writing on an assigned topic. Allowing a child to use a scribe or computer could make all the difference, in that he can focus on his ideas, not the physical act of writing.

As with any child, 2e children participate best when the provided curriculum is at the appropriate level. Unfortunately, educators ask highly-gifted learners to repeat already-learned content instead of engaging them in new learning. When this continually happens in a classroom, 2e students cease to participate, and often experience anxiety and increased behavioral issues, which potentially result in trips to the principal office and/or school suspensions, further inhibiting participation. Even if she displays appropriate classroom behavior, the 2e student will likely lose interest in school when her day feels filled with repetition and unchallenging content. Families with 2e children often cite these issues when turning to homeschooling.

Whether an introvert or extrovert, the homeschooled 2e child should be allowed to appropriately express her likes and dislikes with the curriculum. Homeschooling parents know that the home environment provides a comfortable space for the 2e child to speak up and explore. With input from their children, these parents adjust the schedule to meet the needs of the family, including breaks when their children's interest wanes. Classroom teachers should allow their 2e students the same opportunity to express their dissatisfaction or satisfaction with the curriculum. Though much less able to adapt, teachers will learn more about their students' interests and abilities, and perhaps discover creative ways to engage their 2e students. At the very least, teachers will keep the lines of communication open by encouraging this type of participation.

For the 2e child to have a chance to succeed in a traditional school setting, he must witness his teacher participating in his best interest. He must see her connection with him in her expressions and nonverbal communication. Many 2e children are acutely sensitive and sense insincerity. A genuine relationship is one of the educator's best tools when working with any student, but especially the 2e student.

Underachievement

When teachers do not fully understand the characteristics of gifted children, they find it surprising that an underachieving student may actually have the highest IQ in the class. Educators often mislabel 2e students, focusing on their deficits instead of their strengths, trying to fix perceived laziness, while questioning or disregarding the students' giftedness. (See "Frequently Asked Questions" and "Educate.")

Twice-exceptional learners often deal with underachievement. They may have undiagnosed learning disabilities, be paralyzed by perfectionism and inflexible thinking, or be attempting to fit in with classmates by dimming their brightest skills. Efforts to understand the dynamics of underachievement and loss of potential should receive priority. Consider the 2e child who spends much of his energy maintaining his composure in a sensory overloaded classroom, and thus has nothing left to give when it comes to the academics. Or the 2e child who learns best when moving around, but must sit still in the classroom. Just like the adults who know and love them, 2e children often find aligning their difficulties with their giftedness confusing.

Social Participation

You may find that your 2e students often choose not to participate in social situations. A 2e child may complain that the other children do not share her interests or want to delve into topics as deeply. Social anxiety or poor communication skills also play into this isolation. Concerned parents cite past negative social experiences, classmates not following the game rules, and intimidation over delayed physical skills as reasons their children opt out of recess and afterschool activities. On the other hand, some twice-exceptional learners simply find social interaction uninteresting, while others long to engage but first take time to observe the interactions in class or at recess.

Just as homeschooling parents and classroom teachers must teach what academic participation looks like, they should offer guidance to 2e children as to what social participation looks like. Joining a group, starting and maintaining a reciprocal conversation, and sharing friends with others are some of the social skills which can require modeling. Consider role-playing different situations with the 2e child. Parents likely have a better idea of the specific barriers which interfere with social participation, which makes reviewing the Parent Survey (see "Investigate") and taking time to build the teacher/student relationship vital to this process.

Mentors

Twice-exceptional children benefit from relationships with like-minded individuals or those interested in similar passions, with less of a focus on same-age peers. Because of this, a mentor can be a meaningful addition to a 2e child's life.

Once a child's understanding of a particular interest surpasses a parent's knowledge, mentors often come into play. A successful mentorship requires two components: the mentor-to-student relationship and the opportunity to pursue an area of interest to the student. Outside experts encourage 2e children to push through struggles to help them go farther than they would alone. For example, a child whose skill set with coding and gaming surpasses his parents' may continue to teach himself, but a mentor will invigorate the child's learning and interest. Mentors act as teachers, guides, and colleagues, sharing the same passion and interest as the 2e child. Find great mentors through friends, co-workers, online groups, local colleges, trade schools, or experts in the fields of interests.

Parent Participation

One of my favorite quotes about parent participation comes from Diane Kennedy and Rebecca Banks' book, *Bright Not Broken*: "As parents, we have a responsibility to embrace our children's giftedness and discover ways to nurture their strengths and abilities. At the same time, we must advocate for them in their areas of weakness." [1]

Parents of twice-exceptional learners find themselves working to balance the academic highs and lows, as well as manage their child's unique social and emotional needs. While all parents do this to some extent, the intensities, sensitivities, and extremes of the 2e child keep their parents actively participating.

When parents present their twice-exceptional child with interesting learning opportunities and encourage them to take control, the child's appetite for knowledge can seem endless. Working side by side pursing these inquiries provides a wonderful opportunity to build the parent/child relationship.

Because of the intensities and extremes, parents of 2e children need to connect with and find ways to participate in this community. Gifted- and 2e-specific Facebook groups help with questions and reassure you that you are not alone. Fellow group members celebrate successes and commiserate over struggles. I have listed some of my favorites in the resource section to get you started. For local support, search using keywords such as "gifted," "twice-exceptional," or "homeschooling," plus your state or city. Many groups are closed groups so you must ask to join. Additionally, GHF: Gifted Homeschoolers Forum maintains a list of local support groups on their website.

I have found these groups supportive and safe places to ask questions, as well as share struggles and successes. That is how I found

Celi Trépanier, author of *Educating Your Gifted Child: How One Public School Teacher Embraced Homeschooling*. As she explained about her move from the traditional classroom: "The toll it took on our son was not worth the effort and time spent trying to change an unchangeable solution."[2] A sentiment I found validating and reassuring.

Personal Participation

The journey with a 2e child can sometimes be a struggle, tempting parents to overstep along the way. Though understandable, habitually trying to soften challenging situations allows the 2e child to hide from responsibility, potentially affecting his self-esteem.

As your twice-exceptional child matures, allow her to participate in and developmentally appropriate decisions. Over time, parents should expect their 2e children to participate in planning the daily schedule, choosing new curricula, and determining how to demonstrate understanding of materials. As the 2e child grows accustomed to reflecting whether she is involved in her own learning and if not, what is standing in her way, she will learn to self-advocate, increasing her chances of success as she moves toward adulthood.

> *Tell me and I forget. Teach me and I remember. Involve me and I learn.*
>
> ~Benjamin Franklin

Boost Strategy 10: Evaluate

When it is obvious that the goals cannot be reached, don't adjust the goals, adjust the action steps.

~Confucius

The "Evaluate" *Boost* strategy provides the important players with valuable information by appraising actions and interventions in a careful and thoughtful way. Though intrinsic to "Evaluate," the "thoughtful way" part sometimes seems absent when educators consider twice-exceptional learners. This happens because of the lack of education around 2e students. In order to better support our gifted students with learning disabilities or accommodation needs, frequent and effective evaluation must be part of the ongoing evaluation. After all, no one wants to keep doing something that is truly not working.

Why Evaluate?

Teachers and parents continually evaluate lessons, reflect back on particular days, and consider unexpected outcomes. This process accords teachers and homeschooling parents insight to what things should be done differently or replicated. Without this evaluation, homeschooling parents, teachers, and students struggle to know if learning is taking place. Evaluating what has been learned from informal and formal assessments, including anecdotal notes, provides a map that lays out where to go next and what turns must take place in order for students to reach the desired destination. Understandably, some parents are cautious when formal testing is suggested for their 2e child, concerned about labels as a result of those tests, and question if the testing provides accurate information about their child's knowledge and skills. Other times, school personnel are the ones reluctant to test, especially if a child is producing grade-level work, not realizing that the school's standards may be far below the 2e child's potential.

Parents interested in pursuing an evaluation process should communicate with educators what they have noticed that raises concerns and could indicate a hidden disability. Consider this an opportunity to educate others about the possibility of undiagnosed learning difficulties or social and emotional needs. The early evaluation and identification of the 2e gifted child can be particularly helpful in addressing problems otherwise overlooked. This can save the child years of frustration and prevent plummeting self-esteem.[1]

Evaluate the Why

Some homeschooling parents never considered public school for their children. From the beginning, they wanted to be solely responsible for their child's education. However, a large percentage of homeschooling families who have contacted me through Facebook forums or my blog, MyTwiceBakedPotato.com, started in the traditional public school setting, but turned to homeschooling only after ongoing stress and anxiety became overwhelming for their twice-exceptional child.

After years of such accounts, a common thread in the parents' frustration appeared: school personnel did not question *why* certain behaviors took place, but instead focused only on the resulting behavior. Incidents, such as a 2e student lashing out at another student after receiving repeated pokes in the back during class, or a teacher reprimanding a 2e student after hearing unkind comments without knowing that the "victim" had publicly excluded the 2e student, or a student becoming uncooperative after being required to read a book she already read and did not find interesting the first time around, were dealt with as the 2e child's problem, not as part of a larger concern.

Understandably, parents grow frustrated when educators seem unable to view their 2e child as anything beyond his heightened emotions and outbursts. Educators and administration do not act with malicious intent, but as an ongoing result of misinformation and mislabeling. Teachers, administration, and support staff need to step back and "evaluate the why" of a behavior, especially for the twice-exceptional children who struggle with communication, anxiety, sensory overload, and/or boredom, and who need educated experts in their corner. Considering what took place prior to an incident, with the intent of finding solutions for the future, will help maintain a trusting relationship with this student. This holds true not only for school settings, but for when challenges develop during homeschooling.

When schools ignore the whys, parents in turn must evaluate their options. Many choose to advocate, but if that falls short, they will evaluate the positives and negatives of staying in an environment that may seem detrimental to their child's self-esteem, leading them to consider alternatives, such as homeschooling.

Evaluate the Effectiveness

For effective evaluations, teachers and homeschooling parents should use pre-assessment data. Consider having the student take the chapter test before delivering any instruction and use this information to guide your instruction. If the student does well, the student should not cover the material again. If the student misses questions, the teacher knows what to cover. Grouping students with like skills into smaller groups for instruction, instead of relying on a traditional one-size-fits-all approach, aids this process.

Homeschooling parents and classroom teachers should consider that "current skill levels" mean more than just academics; they include social and emotional strengths and weaknesses, as well. For the 2e student, delayed social and emotional skills can hinder his ability to shine academically, especially when these deficits consume too much energy and force learning to take a back seat to mere coping. Evaluation by outside therapists, such as behavioral, occupational, and

SLPs, can provide important information about the 2e child's social and emotional skills.

During the evaluation process, avoid combining various test scores. Combining the highs and lows erases the true impact of a 2e child's asynchronous development and prevents students from getting the support they need. It also perpetuates the idea that children with high IQs must be equally talented across all subject areas. If her gifts overcompensate for her struggles, her needs are hidden. If her struggles lessen her gifts, then her giftedness is questioned. Instead, look at individual data points to help tease out the 2e child's strengths and weaknesses and arrive at better understanding and support.

Though homeschooling families may have more flexibility with scheduling than classroom teachers, all educators should regularly reflect on their students' progress and evaluate whether their current strategies have been effective. Not only should IEP-protected accommodations be evaluated and adjusted, but informal accommodations should also be frequently evaluated for the presence of patterns. For example, perhaps math works better after lunch or a physical break between reading and science results in greater success with both subject areas.

Self-Evaluation

All students should learn self-reflection and self-evaluation of their work. But as 2e children often work more independently, they need to learn this skill earlier. The influencing adults in the 2e child's life should help him consider academic, social, and emotional growth, as well as effective time management and organization skills as part of his self-reflection and evaluation. Stamina, persistence, and recovery should also be evaluated, since these traits will impact all areas of his life.

Remember that the twice-exceptional child is often his own worst critic. Gifted children with a significant scatter of abilities, whether learning disabled or not, are at risk for self-esteem problems because they tend to evaluate their self-worth heavily against what they cannot do, as opposed to how well they have progressed.[2] Homeschooling parents and classroom teachers should remind the 2e child to focus on progress instead of perseverating on missing skills or incomplete assignments. Over time, this can help the twice-exceptional student feel more positive on harder days and build valuable self-esteem.

Evaluation as a Team

Whether you are a homeschooling parent or a classroom teacher, evaluation should not take place without first considering the twice-exceptional child's thoughts. This team approach builds a positive, respectful relationship. If homeschooling families have experienced a strain on the parent-child relationship due to stress or misunderstanding about the causes for ongoing struggles, they will benefit from implementing team evaluation. Like all children, the 2e child feels valued when he feels heard by the adults in his life.

Frequently discuss the shortcomings and the successes of current skills and practices. Ideally, this would be a reciprocal sharing of thoughts, not one person dominating the discussion. Possible topics for these conversations include:

- What is going well? What is challenging?

- What do you feel the most proud about?

- Is there a different way you would like to show your understanding?

- How can I help you with that?

Tone and intent are important during these meetings. Do not use this time to place blame, but instead to consider current levels and needed adjustments. The 2e learner's comfort during the initial meeting will impact his willingness to participate in future conversations. Lead with positives before starting on the suggestions for improvement.

As this evaluation team builds trust and respect, the teacher and student should understand that whatever is not working can be adjusted. Remain flexible as you evaluate student progress and next steps. Take time to acknowledge growth instead of just looking at pitfalls. This team approach to evaluation will help parents, teachers, and the student feel more positive and empowered when it comes to the learning process.

> *Without reflection, we go blindly on our way, creating more unintended consequences, and failing to achieve anything useful.*
>
> ~Margaret J. Wheatley

Boost Strategy 11: Negotiate

We cannot negotiate with people who say what's mine is mine and what's yours is negotiable.

~John F. Kennedy

Because they are often inflexible, twice-exceptional learners may find negotiating with peers, teachers, and parents challenging. This increases the difficulty of making and keeping friends for this particular population, making "Negotiate" an important *Boost* skill.

The goal of negotiation is for people with disparate desires to arrive at a compromise. With a successful negotiation, all parties gain something while letting go of something else for the good of the group. Ideally, the negotiations will resolve to the satisfaction of all participants.

Characteristics that Encourage Negotiating

Although most children will attempt to negotiate a later bedtime or another cookie at one time or another, negotiating seems to be prominent part of many 2e students' days. *Smart Kids with Learning Difficulties: Overcoming Obstacles and Realizing Potential* lists some of the 2e characteristics which help explain why negotiating with a twice-exceptional child can be challenging:

- Strong questioning attitudes; may appear disrespectful when questioning information, facts, etc. presented by teacher

- Sometimes appear immature because they may use anger, crying, or withdraw to express feelings and to deal with difficulties

- Require frequent teacher support and feedback in deficit areas, highly independent in other areas; often appear to be extremely stubborn and inflexible[1]

Persistent negotiating can challenge parents and teachers. Worse yet, relentless negotiating will continue if a parent or teacher gives in to the student's demands in order to end the negotiating. This temporary solution means that next time the 2e child engages in negotiating tactics, he will likely stand his ground even longer in hopes that the adult will again retreat rather than stay and battle.

Negotiating with Others

Some parents, including myself, tend to fall back on the "because I said so" approach we experienced as children. But my son quickly taught me that this was ineffective with him. It took time, but I realized that his giftedness, sensitivities, and twice-exceptionality demanded a new approach. I had to allow my son to voice his opinions and I had to accept that a certain amount of negotiating would take place.

In order to maintain a positive relationship with the 2e child, pick your battles instead of standing firm on every topic. Focus on solutions instead of getting bogged down in the smaller details. During the negotiating, parents and teachers should communicate their hope for a win-win scenario for all involved. Approach negotiations with empathy. As the adult, remember that most everyone has experienced a time where they have struggled with a compromise.

When Negotiating Fails

I would love to say that negotiating always ends well, that opposing views come together and agree on a compromise no matter what. As we all know, this is not the case. For whatever reason, some days, communication fails and patience runs thin. Parents of 2e children cite many reasons for challenging days, such as growth spurts, tiredness, food sensitivities, communication struggles, and anxiety.

When faced with challenging situations, do not continue engaging once negotiations fall apart and emotions escalate. Assuming that everyone can remain safe and no one is in danger, remove yourself from the argument and wait until the outburst has run its course. This argument does not represent everything about this 2e child, nor does it represent your entire student/teacher relationship.

During the calmer moments, set the tone for a new discussion. What caused the frustration? How could I have helped? What could we do next time? The goal of this conversation should be fact-finding, not reopening negotiations or casting blame.

Negotiate as a Skill

In the heat of the moment, parents and educators may question the value of negotiating. Yet, once emotions have subsided, you will see the benefits. Reframe the ability to negotiate as a skill, instead of labeling it an annoyance, then approach teaching and practicing negotiation skills with respect and empathy. (To refresh your understanding of reframing, see the "Separate" strategy.) Remember that the skill of negotiation includes learning how to accept another person's point of view, even when it differs from your own, and especially when expressed by someone younger than you.

> *In a negotiation, we must find a solution that pleases everyone, because no one accepts that they must lose and that the other must win . . . Both must win!*
>
> ~Nabil N. Jamal

Boost Strategy 12: Appreciate

It's not what you look at that matters, it's what you see.

~Henry David Thoreau

Many twice-exceptional children and their families have not felt appreciated in their traditional brick-and-mortar schools. We cannot continue to say as educators, as parents, as a country that we appreciate differences when we perpetuate sameness as core educational values. While walking in a line or using an inside voice may be necessary for the containment of a large group, placing the utmost importance on compliance does not encourage divergent thinking among our students, let alone our brightest.

Instead, educators, parents, and policymakers must work to shift beliefs and celebrate our students' distinct differences. We must act so that creativity and diversity are encouraged. Integrating "Appreciate," the final *Boost* strategy, will affect such change to the status quo and create the support our 2e learners deserve.

Appreciate Them as Students

Families have sat through frustrating conversations and endless meetings, only to endure continued focus on their children's struggles, not their gifts. A thriving school experience seems impossible to many of these families. While unacceptable for our students and detrimental to our society's future, this commonplace experience continues because people cannot appreciate what they do not understand.

As a veteran teacher, I appreciate the skills needed to teach a large group of learners with varying abilities. I purposefully use a variety of techniques to gain students' attention in order to deliver important information and work to maintain a classroom environment conducive to meeting with small groups and provide individualized instruction. How do you show appreciation for all your students, no matter their learning style? Does your schedule allow for individual and group work? Do social students have specified times to express themselves and share their ideas? Can introverted students demonstrate their knowledge differently? Can students escape to a quieter part of the room if group work becomes intolerable? Do your verbal and nonverbal communications show appreciation for those students who have struggled in other classroom environments?

Through blog discussions and forums, parents share that their children come home from school exhausted by the number of transitions, the overwhelming amount of sensory processing, and the many complicated aspects of the social relationships. Parents should appreciate these challenges when considering afternoon responsibilities or the reasons for emotional outbursts, as should educators, who need to adapt the classroom environment to accommodate these students.

Rather than focusing on the end results, teachers and parents can demonstrate "Appreciate" by praising a student's efforts. Educators should lead with empathy when considering the energy that 2e learner requires to adjust to frequent transitions and often uncomfortable sensory situations. All students should feel safe and comfortable; some students require more accommodations than others to make this happen. Twice-exceptional students deserve educators who celebrate differences, uniqueness, and divergent thinking.

Show appreciation for individual students by considering each student an "expert" in something specific. Depending on the makeup and comfort level of the class, teachers can recognize excellent helpers, talented artists, creative problem-solvers, or caring friends.

Acknowledge every student and students will value the designations, seeing the expert status as genuine.

The twice-exceptional child's determination to share her depth of knowledge can be hard to see as a gift when it makes transitions and time restrictions difficult. Because of their preoccupations with their own interests, these children and adolescents appear more self-centered.[1] While influencing adults can appreciate the quest for answers and meaningful work, they should also appreciate the persistence and inflexibility that can be part of that exploration.

Appreciate Them as Children

I imagine that most readers can remember a time when they wanted to fit in with others, whether in school or even as an adult. No matter when these feelings took over, consider the emotions and focus that "fitting in" took. When parents and trusted teachers demonstrate with their words and actions their acceptance of differences, children feel supported. For any child, but especially for the often intense and emotional 2e child, this appreciation can offset being an outsider.

Parents and educators should work to appreciate those characteristics often labeled as "challenging." Remember the section about reframing in the "Separate" strategy? Reframe a child's stubbornness as determination, a valuable trait. Reframe a student's obsession with a particular subject as a thirst for deep understanding, another valuable trait. Share your appreciation for skills gained and progress made. Communicate your appreciation often, since positive information may go unnoticed by the perfectionist 2e child.

To fully appreciate a child's twice-exceptionality, parents must let go of their own preconceived ideas about their child. Honestly, I struggled with this. Before my son attended school, I assumed that he would love all that school had to offer. I expected him to make friends with kids in the neighborhood, like I had. I imagined watching him participate in team sports, learning to be a good sport despite the outcome of the game. Unfortunately, this was not my family's experience. In the end, I let go of my expectations and moved toward appreciating my son as an individual.

Appreciate Them as Asynchronous Learners

Gifted and talented programs in schools should be led by teachers who understand the differences between previous definitions of "gifted students" and the asynchronous qualities of 2e learners. Show appreciation for 2e children's unique social and emotional needs by creating a balance between cooperative and independent lessons. This will honor those 2e children who are gifted intellectually, but may not be gifted in communicating and negotiating with others.

If you find yourself homeschooling your child, appreciate that not all families feel able to follow your departure. Other frustrated parents keep their 2e children in classrooms for real or assumed restrictions. Many cite financial or time restrictions, while others admit to insecurities about being capable of challenging their child. Let us appreciate our differences as parents within the 2e community and work together for better understanding and education of these special children.

Appreciate Them as a Society

As with any systemic change, educating society about 2e children takes the dedication and action of many, not just a vocal few. Whether we realize it or not, 2e children touch the lives of everyone. We should all strive for their education.

James J. Gallagher shares this idea beautifully: "How can we measure the Sonata unwritten, the curative drug undiscovered, the absence of political insights? They are the difference between what we are and what we could be as a society."[2]

The privilege of a lifetime is being who you are.

~Joseph Campbell

Recommended Resources

Books

Living with Intensity: Understanding the Sensitivity, Excitability, and the Emotional Development of Gifted Children, Adolescents, and Adults
Susan Daniels and Michael M. Piechowski (Great Potential Press)

Genius Denied: How to Stop Wasting Our Brightest Young Minds
Bob Davidson and Jan Davidson (Simon & Schuster)

Writing Your Own Script: The Parent's Role in the Social Development of the Gifted Child
Corin Barsily Goodwin and Mika Gustavson (GHF Press)

Bright Not Broken: Gifted Kids, ADHD, and Autism
Diane M. Kennedy and Rebecca S. Banks, with Temple Grandin (Jossey-Bass)

Different Minds: Gifted Children with AD/HD, Asperger Syndrome, and Other Learning Deficits
Diedre V. Lovecky (Jessica Kingsley Publishing)

When the Labels Don't Fit: A New Approach to Raising A Challenging Child
Barbara Probst (Three Rivers Press)

The Element : How Finding Your Passion Changes Everything
Ken Robinson, with Lou Aronica (Penguin Books)

Educating Your Gifted Child: How One Public School Teacher Embraced Homeschooling
Celi Trépanier (GHF Press)

Smart Kids With Learning Difficulties: Overcoming Obstacles and Realizing Potential
Rich Weinfeld, Linda Barnes-Robinson, Sue Jeweler, and Betty Roffman Shevitz (Prufock Press)

Facebook
2e Seattle
https://www.facebook.com/groups/2eseattle

Gifted Homeschoolers Forum
https://www.facebook.com/GiftedHomeschoolersForum

Homeschool/Online Schooling with Gifted/ 2e Students
https://www.facebook.com/groups/giftedhomeonlineschool/

Twice Exceptional Children (2e)
https://www.facebook.com/groups/158474124337015/

Websites and Additional Information
2e Twice-Exceptional Newsletter
www.2enewsletter.com

Davidson Institute for Talent Development
www.davidsongifted.org

GHF: Gifted Homeschoolers Forum
www.giftedhomeschoolers.org

National Association for Gifted Children (NAGC)
www.nagc.org

Supporting Emotional Needs of the Gifted (SENG)
www.SENGifted.org

Endnotes

Frequently Asked Questions

1. "Glossary of Terms: Asynchrony," *National Association for Gifted Children*, Accessed September 30, 2017, http://www.nagc.org/resources-publications/resources/glossary-terms.

2. "Glossary of Terms: Overexcitability," *National Association for Gifted Children*, Accessed September 30, 2017, http://www.nagc.org/resources-publications/resources/glossary-terms.

3. "The Columbus Group," *Gifted Development Center*, Accessed August 29, 2017, http://www.gifteddevelopment.com/isad/columbus-group.

4. Diane M. Kennedy, Rebecca S. Banks, with Temple Grandin, *Bright Not Broken: Gifted Kids, ADHD, and Autism* (San Francisco: Jossey-Bass, 2011), 183.

Why is Any of This Important?

1. Joan Brasher, "Are gifted children getting lost in the shuffle?" *Research News@Vanderbilt*, January 6, 2014, http://news.vanderbilt.edu/2014/01/gifted-children-study/.

2. Ken Robinson, with Lou Aronica, *The Element: How Finding Your Passion Changes Everything* (New York: Penguin Books, 2009), 9.

Boost Strategy 4: Separate

1. Barbara Probst, *When the Labels Don't Fit : A New Approach to Raising a Challenging Child* (New York: Three Rivers Press, 2008), 109.

2. Probst, *When the Labels Don't Fit*, 82.

Boost Strategy 5: Anticipate

1. Susan Daniels and Michael M. Piechowski, *Living With Intensity: Understanding the Sensitivity, Excitability, and the Emotional Development of Gifted Children, Adolescents, and Adults* (Scottsdale, AZ: Great Potential Press, 2009), 147.

Boost Strategy 6: Accommodate

1. Bob Davidson and Jan Davidson, *Genius Denied: How to Stop Wasting Our Brightest Young Mind* (New York: Simon & Schuster, 2004), 159.

Boost Strategy 7: Accelerate

1. "Glossary of Terms: Curriculum Compacting," *National Association for Gifted Children*, Accessed October 2, 2017, http://www.nagc.org/resources-publications/resources/glossary-terms.

2. "What research says about the value of homework: Research review," *The Center for Public Education*, February 5, 2007, http://www.centerforpubliceducation.org/Main-Menu/instruction/What-research-says-about-the-value-of-homework-At-a-glance/What-research-says-about-the-value-of-homework-Research-review.htnl?css=print#sthash.AY4WPFxe.dpuf.

Boost Strategy 8: Fascinate

1. Robinson, *The Element*, 116.

2. Kennedy, et al, *Bright Not Broken*, 198.

Boost Strategy 9: Participate

1. Kennedy, et al, *Bright Not Broken*, 16.

2. Celi Trépanier, *Educating Your Gifted Child: How One Public School Teacher Embraced Homeschooling* (Olympia, WA: GHF Press, 2015), 15.

Boost Strategy 10: Evaluate

1. James T. Webb, Edward R. Amend, Nadia E. Webb, Jean Goerss, Paul Beljan, and F. Richard Olenchat, *Misdiagnosis and Dual Diagnoses of Gifted Children and Adults: ADHD, Bipolar, OCD, Asperger's, Depression, and Other Disorders* (Scottsdale, AZ: Great Potential Press, 2005), 156.

2. Webb, et al, *Misdiagnosis and Dual Diagnoses of Gifted Children and Adults*, 145.

Boost Strategy 11: Negotiate

1. Rich Weinfeld, Linda Barnes-Robinson, Sue Jeweler, and Betty Roffman Shevitz, *Smart Kids With Learning Difficulties: Overcoming Obstacles and Realizing Potential* (Waco, TX: Prufock Press, 2006), 31.

Boost Strategy 12: Appreciate

1. Diedre V. Lovecky, *Different Minds: Gifted Children with AD/HD, Asperger Syndrome, and Other Learning Deficits* (Philadelphia: Jessica Kingsley Publishing, 2005), 127.

2. *The Twice Exceptional Dilemma* (Washington, DC: National Education Association, 2006), copyright page, http://www.nea.org/assets/docs/twiceexceptional.pdf.

About the Author

Kelly Hirt is a public school teacher, homeschooling parent, blogger, and writer of both fiction and nonfiction works. She has taught elementary school for twenty-five years in Washington State. During that time she has had the pleasure to serve as a student teacher mentor, district level trainer, and an active member during leadership teams and curriculum adoption reviews.

Kelly became a reluctant homeschooling parent and activist after the traditional public school system to which she dedicated her professional life failed her twice-exceptional son.

She started her blog, My Twice Baked Potato (MyTwiceBakedPotato.com), to educate parents and connect with other families who found themselves parenting a twice-exceptional child.

Kelly lives near Seattle and enjoys writing, watching movies, going for walks with her family, and playing various video games with her tech-savvy son.

Made in the USA
Lexington, KY
21 April 2018